IMAGES
of America

CHINESE IN BOSTON

1870–1965

Chinatown, Harrison Ave., Boston, Mass.

HARRISON AVENUE, C. 1907–1915. This famous postcard image portrays a street-level view of Harrison Avenue, north from Beach Street, in the heart of today's Boston Chinatown. Chinese pedestrians wearing traditional dress and a queue hairstyle are clearly visible in the center. Stores and shops, some of which were owned by Chinese, along with horse-drawn vehicles and electric streetcars, lined both sides of this commercial area after the street was widened in 1894. (Courtesy of Bostonian Society.)

On the cover: CHINESE IN BOSTON TERCENTENARY PARADE, 1930. In celebration of the 300th anniversary of the founding of the City of Boston, the Chinese community participated in the city's parade along the route of Boylston and Tremont Streets. The spectacle of public pageantry reveals a growing recognition of the Chinese presence in the city while leaving the illusion of civic participation among the marginalized Chinese population under the Exclusion Act. (Courtesy of Chinese Historical Society of New England collection.)

IMAGES
of America

CHINESE IN BOSTON

1870–1965

Wing-kai To and the Chinese Historical
Society of New England

ARCADIA
PUBLISHING

Published by Arcadia Publishing
Charleston, South Carolina

Library of Congress Catalog Card Number: 2007930872

For all general information contact Arcadia Publishing at:
Telephone 843-853-2070
Fax 843-853-0044
E-mail sales@arcadiapublishing.com
For customer service and orders:
Toll-Free 1-888-313-2665

Visit us on the Internet at www.arcadiapublishing.com

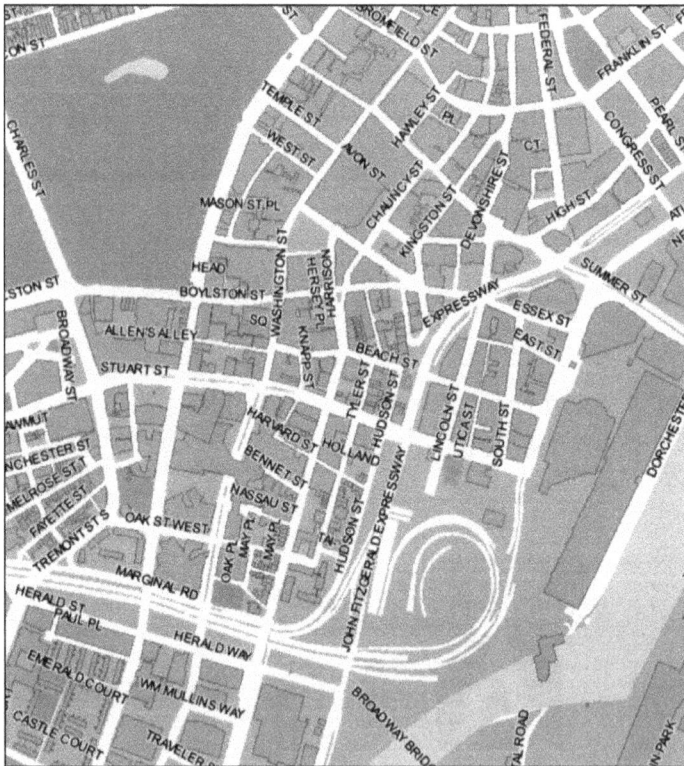

MAP OF BOSTON CHINATOWN. The early development of Boston Chinatown was centered in a small area around Beach Street (shown here), Harrison Avenue (shown here), Oxford Place, and Oxford Street. It eventually extended its boundaries to Essex Street in the north, Washington Street in the west, Marginal Road in the south, and the Rose Kennedy Greenway in the east. (Courtesy of Boston Redevelopment Authority.)

CONTENTS

ACKNOWLEDGMENTS

I have been fortunate to receive the generous support from friends and colleagues in the Chinese Historical Society of New England (CHSNE), who welcomed me to conduct research on their family and community history. My profound gratitude goes to Tunney Lee and David Chang who provided valuable research assistance and wise counsel throughout the project. I also thank Caroline Chang, David Chang, Debbie Dong, Stephanie Fan, Jacquie Kay, Peter Kiang, and Shauna Lo for their generous help in reading and commenting on the manuscript.

I am indebted to the work of previous scholars and community members who laid the foundation for the photograph collection. Doris Chu and the Chinese Culture Institute (later renamed International Society) donated important photographs to CHSNE after publishing *The Chinese in Massachusetts*. David S. Y. Wong, Davis Woo, Peter Chan, Caroline Chang, and Ting Fun Yeh deserve recognition for establishing CHSNE in 1992. Ting Fun Yeh and Stephanie Fan devoted much time and effort to enrich the CHSNE photograph collection. I also benefited from reading the presentations by Arthur Krim on his survey of historical buildings of Chinatown.

This book would not have been possible without the generous donations of photographs and research materials from the following individuals: Carmen Chan, Peter Chan, Ann Chang, Caroline Chang, David Chang, Bill Chin, Frank Chin, May Chin, Josephine Chin, Thomas Chin, Doris Chu, Debbie Dong, Stephanie Fan, Amy Guen, Edward Guen, Peter Kiang, Shue Pon Lee, Tunney Lee, Gary Libby, Catherine Mah, Helen Chin Schlichte, Doris Wong, Dorothy Wong, Lela Wong, Reggie Wong, and Cynthia Yee. I am grateful to them all.

The photographs are also drawn from the following archives and libraries whose staff were especially generous of their time: Boston Athenaeum, Boston Globe, Boston Herald, Boston Public Library, Bostonian Society, Concord Public Library, Connecticut Historical Society, Harvard University Archives, Historic New England, Maine Historical Society, MIT Library, Northfield Mount Hermon School Archive, Peabody Essex Museum, Schlesinger Library at Harvard University, Washington State University Archives, and Wellesley College Archives.

The research of the book is also partially supported by a summer grant from the Center for Academic Research and Teaching at Bridgewater State College and a research fellow position from the Institute for Asian American Studies at the University of Massachusetts at Boston. I am grateful to my wife Charlotte and my daughter Hannah whose love and support helped me endure long hours of scanning photographs and working in Chinatown away from family responsibilities over the summer. Most of all, I dedicate this book to all early Chinese American settlers in New England, before 1965, who helped improve the life of Asian Americans today.

INTRODUCTION

Boston's Chinatown, while small in comparison to New York's and San Francisco's, has maintained a rich history as a vibrant commercial and residential community in the same locale since its initial settlement in the late 1870s. Its continuity in preserving some of the traditional architecture and streetscapes, as well as its enduring character of family and community life, distinguishes Chinatown in Boston as a more coherent community than most others on the East Coast. The local legacy of Chinese Americans is visible both in the ongoing presence of Chinatown, and also in numerous contributions to the development of trade, industry, education, politics, and culture in New England.

Chinese merchants and students first arrived in small towns and communities in New England in the mid-19th century. They owned the earliest Chinese tea shops and restaurants in Boston and Portland, Maine, and some were among the first Chinese to study in missionary schools in western Massachusetts and to graduate from a U.S. college in Connecticut. Many were sojourners who returned to China to contribute to its modernization, while a smaller number stayed as pioneers to acculturate into American life through marriage, education, and missionary activities. With the advent of industrialization and the transcontinental railroad, another stream of immigrant pioneers ventured into New England from across the American West and Canada or through New York. An early group was recruited as strike breakers to work at a shoe factory in North Adams. Almost all of these male workers came from Toisan County of Guangdong Province in China from which there was a constant flow of migrant labor to the United States through the contract system.

When Chinese laborers found their way from North Adams to Boston after the 1870s, they settled in the South Cove landfill area where immigrant Irish, Italian, Jewish, and Syrian workers had previously established successive ethnic enclaves following the opening of the nearby South Station railroad hub in the 1840s. By the dawn of the 20th century, several hundred Chinese resided along narrow alleys such as Oxford Place and Oliver Place, adjacent to the two main roads of Harrison Avenue and Beach Street. Although some were ignored or ridiculed by other immigrants, most Chinese were spared the violence and forced removal that occurred on the West Coast when Congress passed the 1882 Chinese Exclusion Act. An immigration raid in Boston Chinatown in 1903, however, reduced the population of Chinese residents in the neighborhood by nearly half. The population did not rebound until after the second decade of the 20th century. Throughout this period, working and living conditions were deplorable. The widening of Harrison Avenue in 1893 almost destroyed the city's Chinese business core. The elevated transit railway also created unbearable noise and pollution when it passed through the neighborhood from 1899 to 1941. Through perseverance, some Chinese found their niche by establishing successful laundries and restaurants between 1900 and 1930. This enabled the boundaries of Chinatown to expand across Tyler Street, Hudson Street, Harrison Avenue, and Beach Street.

As Chinese merchants and workers clustered around the city and scattered across the region, they developed organizations and services based in Chinatown for recreation, information, and support. The first groups were tongs—clan associations with the dubious image of engaging in illicit activities such as gambling, opium smoking, and extortion. By the second decade of the 20th century, some community leaders established the Chinese Consolidated Benevolent Association of New England and the Chinese Merchants Association to represent Chinatown. Many families, including those with surnames such as Moy, Yee, Chin, Wong, and Lee, formed their own family associations in the 1920s. Since many earlier settlers were single men or had left their wives behind in China, the family associations provided an extended kinship structure for the "bachelor society" similar to that of a fraternity or sworn brotherhood. Those who were later able to bring their wives and establish families in Chinatown created a new second-generation culture beginning in the 1920s. These children who were born in the United States or who immigrated at young ages typically attended the local Quincy School and spoke both English and Toisanese. Although they interacted with Syrian immigrants and other non-Chinese children in public school, many found social support in the 1930s in organizations that focused on Chinatown youth such as the Quong Kow Chinese School and its marching band, the YMCA, and the local Boy Scout troop.

One notable development was the emergence of a strong organizational culture for Chinese American girls and women in the 1930s. The Chinese Mission and the Denison House were both active in recruiting immigrant women and girls to help spread the gospel while instilling a collective sense of self-worth. They organized a girls' basketball team and other leisure activities for Chinese women. The Catholic Maryknoll Sisters Center also became quite active after being established in 1946. Many Chinese American women in the 1930s joined Chinatown organizations that strove to support a strong and independent China. The most prominent example was the New England Chinese Women's Association founded in 1940, whose members were highly visible in raising funds to support China against Japanese imperialism during World War II. Some women such as Rose Lok, the first Chinese American female pilot in Boston, were pioneers who joined the Chinese Patriotic Flying Corps. In 1952, a Chinese American mother in Maine, Toy Len Goon, was honored as Mother of the Year.

Chinese in Boston were politically active in the late 1930s and early 1940s primarily in response to the turmoil in China. They often expressed their nationalism toward China through street parades and demonstrations. The war also imparted a sense of U.S. patriotism and civic participation in Chinese American students. From their war experience, Chinese Americans gained new respect through their heroism in U.S. military units such as the 14th Air Service Group.

Chinese American community life in Boston during the postwar period from 1945 through the 1970s was characterized by the threatening impact of urban redevelopment and expanding opportunities for interaction outside of Chinatown. Specific challenges came from the construction of the Central Artery and the extension of the Massachusetts Turnpike highways in the 1950s and 1960s—which displaced hundreds of Chinese American families on Hudson Street and Albany Street—followed by aggressive institutional expansion by Tufts University and the New England Medical Center in the 1970s. Given Chinatown's proximity to downtown Boston, intense pressures of land redevelopment have persisted to the present, forcing community members to establish new civic organizations and strategies to defend as well as develop Chinatown in ways that enable its rich legacy not only to survive, but thrive.

In the 1980s, a Chinatown gate and community murals represented new public symbols to demonstrate Chinatown's dynamic cultural identity and historical importance. More recently, a memorial was completed in 2007 to honor hundreds of Chinese immigrant pioneers buried in Boston's Mount Hope Cemetery. Although the future of Boston Chinatown may be difficult to determine, its historical record is visible and deserves to be recognized. This book, then, is our collective effort to make such recognition possible—to preserve the legacy of Chinese Americans in Boston and New England, especially prior to 1965, and to honor the vitality of their continuing history.

One

ARRIVALS IN NEW ENGLAND

CHINESE WORKERS IN SAMPSON SHOE FACTORY, NORTH ADAMS, 1870. The earliest presence of Chinese workers in Massachusetts is widely recognized as the group of 75 who were hired by Calvin T. Sampson to break a labor strike and work in his shoe factory in North Adams. This group portrait outside the factory belies the arduous journey they undertook from the West Coast and the hostile reception they received from striking workers. Some of these Chinese workers possibly constituted the early Chinese settlement in the Boston area. (Courtesy of Boston Athenaeum.)

LAI BEN VILLAGE, TOISAN COUNTY, 1970S. Toisan (Taishan) County of Guangdong Province is the location of most of the ancestral villages for Chinese who immigrated to Boston from the 1870s to the 1960s. This photograph, taken in the 1970s, depicts a view of pond, communal well, and threshing ground in a Lee family village, from which descendants of Lee Yue arrived in Boston in 1893. (Courtesy of Tunney Lee.)

ANCESTRAL HOME, 2006. Visiting the ancestral villages in Toisan County has helped Chinese Bostonians connect with the memory of their distant ancestors who made the long journey to America. May and Thomas Chin (left) visited May's ancestral village with the help of a local overseas Chinese representative. (Courtesy of May and Thomas Chin.)

10

THE CHINA TEA TRADE, C. 1790–1800. This spectacular illustration of the Whampoa Island in Guangzhou shows the production of tea as well as preparations for its export from the anchorage. After 1787, the first American ship set sail from Massachusetts to the port cities of Whampoa and ushered in the era of America's China trade in New England. (Courtesy of Peabody Essex Museum.)

TRADE BY NEW ENGLAND MERCHANTS IN CANTON (GUANGZHOU), C. 1852. The early steamer *Spark*, seen alongside a small sampan loading chests of tea, was brought to Canton by Capt. Robert Bennett Forbes in 1849. Forbes founded the firm of Russell and Company and left an estate in Milton, known today as Captain Forbes House. Many other notable Bostonians also made their wealth on the China trade. (Courtesy of Peabody Essex Museum and Forbes House Museum.)

CHINAMAN'S TEA STORE.

TWENTY TO FORTY CENTS PER POUND SAVED.

CHOICE PURE TEAS OF ALL KINDS.

FRESH EVERY DAY PURE COFFEE,

CHINESE TEA STORE ADVERTISEMENT IN BOSTON, 1865. This advertisement of a tea store owned by successful merchant Oong Ar-showe at 25 Union Street is the earliest evidence of a Chinese shop in Boston. His advertisement stresses the authenticity of his tea products through text and the image of the loading of tea cargo from the ports. It is interesting to note that he also sold coffee! Oong Ar-showe became a naturalized citizen in 1860, perhaps the first Chinese in Massachusetts to do so, and became well known in Malden, a suburb of Boston. His son William, born in 1854, is most likely the first United States–born Chinese in Massachusetts. (Courtesy of Boston City Directory, 1865.)

354

NEW CHINAMAN'S TEA STORE. NEW TEA AND COFFEE

CHINAMAN'S TEA & COFFEE STORE

From China & Japan to San Francisco, and thence by rail to this city. All goods warranted. Money refunded if goods do not prove as represented.

AR FOO, CHINA Tea Merchant, 333 Congress St.

PORTLAND STONE WARE CO.

Manufacturers of every description of

STONE WARE GOODS,

DOUBLE GLAZED, VITRIFIED,

STONE DRAIN AND WATER PIPE,

Factory, North End of Deering's Bridge.

J. N. WINSLOW, Treasurer.

J. T. WINSLOW, Superintendent.

PORTLAND'S TEA STORE, 1871. Ar Foo Fong went to Portland, Maine, in 1860 to work for George C. Shaw in his store on Middle Street helping customers select teas. By 1871, he had his own store on Congress Street, as evidenced here by his advertisement in the Portland city directory of 1871. (Courtesy of Maine Historical Society.)

THE GREAT CHINESE MUSEUM, 1845. This lithograph depicts exhibits of the Great Chinese Museum at the Marlboro Chapel and reflects the American fascination with China. The images include Chinese emperor Daoguang and his officials, the empress and her ladies-in-waiting, the Chinese judicial system, scholar-officials, opium, merchants and their wives, military men, farmers, craftsmen, and service people, and miscellaneous products of China. It offers a romantic view of China mediated by merchant interests in China. (Courtesy of Boston Athenaeum.)

BURLINGAME DELEGATION IN BOSTON, 1868. The Burlingame Treaty of 1868 acknowledged the right of free emigration of the citizens of both China and America and guaranteed reciprocal privileges of residence, school, and travel. After it was signed in Washington, D.C., the Burlingame Delegation visited other cities, including Boston, where the city hosted a banquet at the St. James Hotel on August 21, 1868. The treaty was later negated by the passing of the Chinese Exclusion Act of 1882, the first time the United States formally excluded a particular ethnic group from entering the country. (Courtesy of Bostonian Society.)

MANDARIN YUNG WING.

YUNG WING'S PORTRAIT, 1878. As American missionaries extended their influence in China, they began to recruit and enroll Chinese students in missionary schools in New England. The most prominent example was Yung Wing, who after studying in Morrison School in Hong Kong, was enrolled in Monson Academy in Massachusetts in 1847. Yung Wing went on to become the first Chinese student to receive a U.S. college degree, from Yale University in 1854. Yung Wing sought to promote modernization of China and helped the Chinese government to send groups of students to study in New England in the 1870s. His efforts were however hindered by both opponents of reforms in China and the anti-Chinese movement in the United States. Yung Wing's contribution is now widely recognized both in China and the United States. This wood-engraved illustration comes from *Harper's Weekly*, May 18, 1878. (Courtesy of Connecticut Historical Society.)

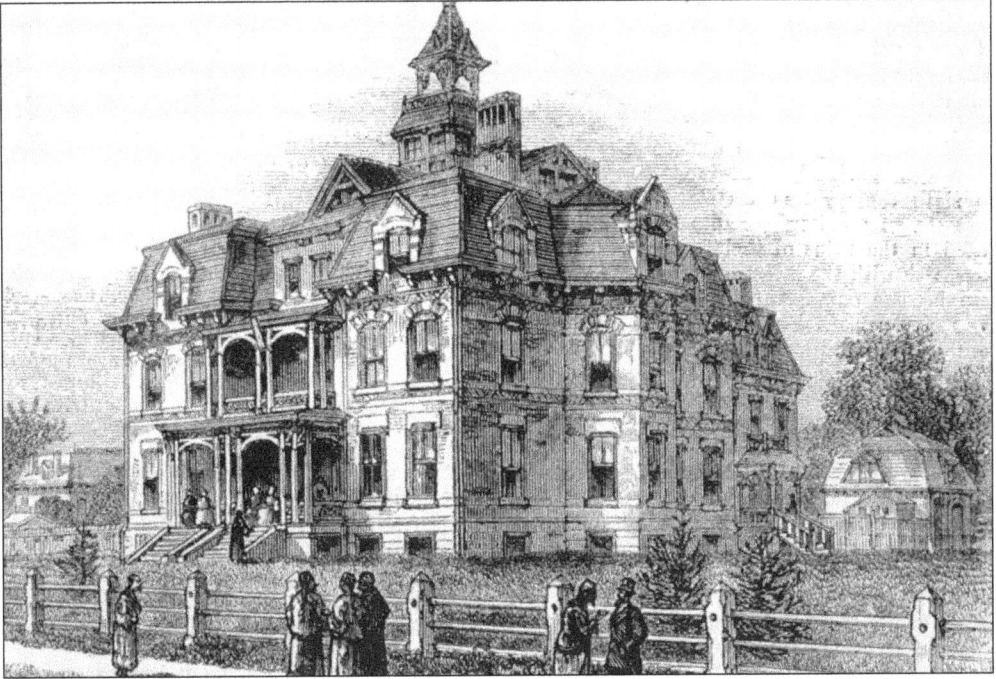

CHINESE EDUCATIONAL MISSION BUILDING, 1878. The Chinese Educational Mission, sponsored by the Chinese government at the urging of Yung Wing, brought 120 students to Hartford, Connecticut, in the 1870s to study Western culture, science, and technology. The program was terminated in 1881 for various political reasons. The building pictured here in *Harper's Weekly* was located at 252 Collins Street and torn down in the 1960s to make way for St. Francis Hospital. (Courtesy of Connecticut Historical Society.)

CHINESE CLASSROOM IN HARTFORD, 1878. *Harper's Weekly* featured the young students, all boys, in their traditional mode of learning, either seated at their desks or standing to talk with their teacher. The Chinese teacher's responsibility was to assure that students would retain their Chinese language and culture in the United States. (Courtesy of Connecticut Historical Society.)

FIRST GROUP OF CHINESE BOYS DEPARTING FOR HARTFORD, 1872. Thirty students are shown in front of the China Merchants Steam Navigation Company in Shanghai before their departure for the Chinese Educational Mission in 1872. The average age of the students was about 12. (Courtesy of Manuscripts, Archives, and Special Collections, Washington State University Libraries.)

REUNION OF THE STUDENTS IN CHINA, 1890. Many of the students had stellar careers upon their return to China. From left to right are (first row) Liang Pao Chew, mining engineer; Li Lai Tong; Kwong King Yang, railroad engineer; Tong Sze Chung, naval officer; and Yen Fu Lee, newspaper editor; (second row) Wong Wai Chung; Jeme Tien Yau, railroad engineer; Chung Mun Yew, railroad director; Tong Kai Son; Kin Ta Ting, doctor; Liang Pao Shi, railway official; Kwong Young Kong, mining engineer; Luk Hin Shen; Willy Tseng; and Liu Yu Lin, consular service. (Courtesy of Manuscripts, Archives, and Special Collections, Washington State University Libraries.)

16

BASEBALL CLUB OF THE CHINESE EDUCATIONAL MISSION BOYS, 1878. Many of the students lived with local families to learn about American customs and activities, including sports. This picture was taken in front of the Chinese Educational Mission headquarters on Collins Street. The boys and their future professions from left to right are (first row) Chun Kee Young, naval doctor; Lee Kwai Pan, tea business in New York; Liang Tun Yen, cabinet officer and minister of foreign affairs; and Kwong Wing Chung, naval officer; (second row) Tsai Shou Kee, director of customs; Chung Ching Shing, interpreter in the United States consular service; Woo Chung Yen, consular service; Jeme Tien Yau, railroad engineer, builder of the Peking-Kalgan railway; and Wong Kai Kah, diplomatic service. (Courtesy of Manuscripts, Archives, and Special Collections, Washington State University Libraries.)

FAMILIES AND CHILDREN OF EARLY STUDENTS, C. 1908. Among the two most famous Chinese Educational Mission students were Tang Shao Yi, who studied at Columbia University before returning to become the first Chinese prime minister of the Republic of China, 1912–1921, and Yung Kwai, who advised the foreign office in the United States and attended both Yale and Columbia Universities. This picture of the children of Tang Shao Yi and Yung Kwai was taken around 1908. (Courtesy of Manuscripts, Archives, and Special Collections, Washington State University Libraries.)

FIRST CHINESE PROFESSOR, 1879. Ko Kun Hua was the first instructor of Chinese language at Harvard University, where he taught from 1879 to 1882. Ko wore Chinese robes appropriate to his official rank, that of a sub-prefect. He arrived in Cambridge in 1879 and died of illness in 1882. (Courtesy of Harvard University Archives.)

CHINESE SUNDAY SCHOOL IN MAINE, C. 1890. This photograph is the earliest evidence of Chinese cutting their queue and assimilating into American social life in Maine. Chinese men joined Christian Sunday schools to learn English and to socialize. This photograph shows Wong My, Sam Sing, and the Chinese Sunday school class of Essie Wills at the South Parish Congregational Church, Augusta, about 1890. (Courtesy of Maine Historical Society.)

CHINESE SUNDAY SCHOOL PICNIC, C. 1925. Members of the Chinese Sunday school of the First Baptist Church of Portland, Maine, are shown here posing with their teachers during a picnic on a Casco Bay island, probably in the mid- to late 1920s. (Courtesy of Gary Libby and Maine Historical Society.)

CHINESE IN NORTHFIELD MOUNT HERMON SCHOOL, 1891. Missionaries in Boston began to recruit arriving Chinese workers to study in Sunday schools in the 1880s. One missionary worker, Mrs. Porter of Allen Street, sent one of her students to Mount Hermon School in western Massachusetts. Chin Loon Teung arrived at the school in 1886 at the age of 20 and spoke at the school's first commencement in June 1887 as a representative of the Asian students at the institution. Following his graduation in 1892, Chin Loon Teung was invited to preach at Holyoke Church. This class picture was taken on the steps of Camp Hall, then the dining hall for the school. (Courtesy of Northfield Mount Hermon School Archive.)

CHINESE GIRLS IN NORTHFIELD SEMINARY, 1924. The Tremont Temple Baptist Church in Boston supported Chinese children who were orphaned or whose parents may have been unable to care for them. Some were sent to Northfield Seminary, the coeducational counterpart to Mount Hermon. Mary Dunn, a girl from a Chinese laundry family, is shown here with the East Hall Dormitory champions of the Northfield Seminary intramural basketball season of 1923–1924. The group is sitting on the front steps of the Margaret Olivia Music Hall at the seminary. (Courtesy of Northfield Mount Hermon School Archive.)

MADAME CHIANG, WELLESLEY COLLEGE, CLASS OF 1917. The most famous early Chinese female student in a New England college was undoubtedly Mei-ling Soong, later married to Generalissimo Chiang Kai-shek. She graduated from Wellesley College in 1916 after transferring from Wesleyan College. In this photograph, Mei-ling Soong is seated in the first row, second from the right, with her class at a 1916 YWCA conference in Silver Bay, New York. (Courtesy of Wellesley College Archives.)

CHINESE WORKERS IN NORTH ADAMS, 1870. This sketch by Theo Davis published in *Harper's Weekly* shows Chinese in the workshop of the Sampson Shoe Factory in North Adams. After the transcontinental railroad was completed in 1869, many Chinese workers moved east in search of jobs and security as anti-Chinese sentiment gathered momentum in California and the Western frontier. (Courtesy of Boston Athenaeum.)

CHINESE WORKER IN WESTERN DRESS, C. 1870. The choice of clothing reflected other conflicts facing the workers who were suddenly immersed in a new culture. Some adopted Western dress, some retained traditional garments. Some incorporated Christianity into their lives, others did not. Some returned to China while others moved to Boston or other parts of New England. (Courtesy of Doris Chu/International Society.)

Two

SETTLEMENT IN BOSTON CHINATOWN

FUNERAL PROCESSION ON HARRISON AVENUE, 1903. Photographer Thomas Marr documented a traditional Chinese funeral on Harrison Avenue for an article by Herbert Heywood in *New England Magazine* in 1905. Chinese mourners and curious non-Chinese spectators overflowed the streets of the early settlement of Boston Chinatown. The crowd was everywhere, on the balconies of buildings as well as on the procession routes. Signage of some of the Chinese stores, such as S. Y. Yuen Groceries, is clearly visible along the street. (Courtesy of Boston Public Library, Print Department; photograph by Thomas Marr.)

HARRISON AVENUE, BEFORE WIDENING, 1893. Photographs documenting the widening of Harrison Avenue were first published in the Annual Report of the Street Laying Out Department for the year 1894, by the Boston Street Commissioners in 1895. This image shows Harrison Avenue, looking north from Beach Street to Essex Street, with the front sides of the buildings on the right being removed to widen the road. The *Boston Globe* reported that the Chinese district, which bordered the right side of the street, might be wiped out by the project but fears subsided after the resurgence of Chinese businesses following the completion of the project. (Courtesy of Boston Athenaeum.)

HARRISON AVENUE, AFTER WIDENING, 1894. This is the view of Harrison Avenue after the widening. The buildings on the right near the corner of Oxford Place (the street that interrupts the block) were mostly Chinese businesses, while the buildings on the left remained non-Chinese. Ten years later, the Boston city directory of 1905 listed many Chinese businesses along Harrison Avenue, Oxford Place, and Beach Street. (Courtesy of Boston Athenaeum.)

TILE OF HONG FAR LOW RESTAURANT, C. 1916. One example of the rebuilding that occurred after the widening is 36–38 Harrison Avenue, the location of what is believed to be the earliest Chinese restaurant in Boston Chinatown. A tiled door step, marking the establishment of the restaurant in 1879, and a second-floor balcony were added, possibly during the building reconstruction in 1896. (Courtesy of CHSNE collection.)

HONG FAR LOW MENU, EARLY 1900S. This menu from the Hong Far Low restaurant in Boston features a picture of a bald man in Chinese dress, with the caption: "This is the first man in Boston who made chop suey in 1879." Such a caption would indicate that the restaurant served non-Chinese patrons. The menu includes this cover image and two pages of menu items. (Courtesy of Harley Spiller.)

The * Chinese * Monthly * News.

Vol. II.

OFFICE, 36 HARRISON AVENUE.

No. 17.

FIFTY CENTS PER YEAR.
SUEY HOENG, Editor, & Publisher.

ENTERED IN THE POST-OFFICE AT BOSTON, AS SECOND-CLASS MATTER.

FIVE CENTS PER COPY.
P. Y. MOY Manager.

FEB. 1, 1892.

J. Maguire   **Burton Ale Vaults**   J.J.Lowell
17 Albany St. Bet. Beach & Kneeland St.

WHITNEY BROS.

A. B. CURRIER,
709 Washington Street, Boston.

PRESCOTT BROS.

LOVELL'S ARMS STORE.
J. P. LOVELL.
147 Washington Street, Boston.

C. A. W. Crosby & Son
474 Washington St. Boston, Mass.

WHITNEY BROS.
63 and 65 Essex Street, Boston.

62 and 64 Cornhill Street,
Near Court St., Boston.

THE CHINESE MONTHLY NEWS, 1892. A monthly newspaper was published by an office at 36 Harrison Avenue, in the same building as the Hong Far Low restaurant. The news was managed by P. Y. Moy, and it sold for 5¢. The paper provided news of China and sold advertisements to an assortment of stores selling liquor, jewels, firearms, hats, and paper items. That a Chinese-language newspaper was printed and sold would indicate a settled Chinese community by 1892, despite the transient nature of many sojourners. (Courtesy of CHSNE collection.)

26

LOCK SEN LOW RESTAURANT, 1901. Another example of an early Chinese restaurant is Lock Sen Low at 44–46 Beach Street. With a clearly visible store sign, the restaurant included a balcony in the Chinese style that wrapped around the building on the south side of Beach and the west side of Harrison Avenue. (Courtesy of Historic New England.)

CHINESE MERCHANTS AT TEA, 1903. Journalist Herbert Heywood and photographer Thomas Marr got a close-up view of the second floor of Bun Fong Low, a teahouse and restaurant on 32 Harrison Avenue. Owners of the restaurants are shown drinking tea in the dining room, adorned with Chinese couplets and fine furniture. (Courtesy of CHSNE collection.)

GRAND DINING ROOM, 1903. The top floor of the same restaurant above was decorated with traditional marble tables and modern light fixtures. The altars were positioned in the middle of the room, a common practice, to honor patron deities of the restaurant. (Courtesy of CHSNE collection.)

MERCHANT WIVES AND CHILDREN, 1920. Chinatown was predominantly a bachelor society in the late 19th and early 20th centuries. Because of the Chinese Exclusion Act, only merchants, not laborers, were allowed to bring their families from China. The few successful merchants with the resources to do so were able to have some semblance of family life in Boston. Here a mother is shown with her three young children. (Courtesy of Boston Public Library, Print Department.)

GENTRY AND MERCHANT, 1903. It was not uncommon for the owner of a store to be an educated man who maintained the lifestyle of a scholarly gentleman with a studio in his home or restaurant. (Courtesy of CHSNE collection.)

TRADITIONAL CHINESE MARRIAGE, c. 1910. Before the 1920s, most merchants followed rituals in China with the husband and the wife posing in the photo studio in a traditional manner. (Courtesy of CHSNE collection.)

BUDDHIST CEREMONY IN FRONT OF HONG FAR LOW, C. 1909. Sons and male descendants of the deceased are responsible for performing most of the funeral rituals. Signage adorns the facades of the buildings with the Hong Far Low restaurant clearly visible. Crowds of people lined Harrison Avenue to watch the ceremony. People can also be seen watching from the second-story windows and balcony of 36 Harrison Avenue. (Courtesy of Bostonian Society.)

FUNERAL ON HARRISON AVENUE, 1903. Funerals were elaborate rituals for Chinese families to fulfill their filial obligations. This close-up view shows the minute detail of offerings and detailed procedures for mourning. The street spectacle was also intended to display the prestige of the deceased and the wealth of the families. (Courtesy of Boston Public Library, Print Department.)

MODERN CHINESE FUNERAL, 1940. Some 30 years after the above period, residents of Chinatown continued to mourn their major leaders in public funeral processions. They replaced traditional clothing and mourning rituals with a more official parade route of dignitaries, friends, and school bands. This was the funeral of businessman Wong Tarn Shiew and was reported in local newspapers. (Courtesy of Faye Soo Hoo.)

CHINATOWN IMMIGRATION RAID, 1903. On October 11, 1903, the police in Boston used the opportunity of a funeral for a murder victim in Chinatown to arrest over 300 men for not carrying proper immigration documents. Eventually over 50 men were deported and over 100 fled the area. The press vividly portrayed how the police officers grabbed the escaping Chinese men by their queues and stepped on them during the arrest. It was the most famous anti-Chinese incident in Boston during the Exclusion era. (Courtesy of CHSNE collection.)

OVER 300 CHINAMEN ARRESTED IN BIG ROUND-UP BY POLICE

10/12/1903 Boston Herald

ROOSEVELT TOO EAGER

Long Declares He Was Anxious to Send a Fleet Against Spain Before War Was Declared.

A SENSATION AT THE CAPITAL.

Former Secretary's Comment in Magazine Likely to Be Resented by President It Is Said.

ATTEMPTED ESCAPE AND RECAPTURE OF CHINAMEN
After the Upsetting of the Wagon on Harrison Avenue.

TONGS DARED DO NO HARM

Police from Chinatown to Grave During Funeral Procession of Wong Yak Chung

Immigration Authorities Determined That All Celestials Who Cannot Show Registration Papers Must Leave Country — Denizens of Chinatown in Frenzy of Fear—Mad Rush to Escape—Prisoners Taken to Federal Building.

BOSTON CHINATOWN RAID, 1935. Although relations between the government and the Chinese community improved in the decades after the immigration raid, the police still regularly raided the neighborhood for suspects of gambling and crime. These four men were detained in a round-up in 1935. (Courtesy of CHSNE collection.)

OXFORD PLACE, 1921. Oxford Place was and still is a narrow street with a series of connected, three-story brick houses where Chinese settlers have lived since the 1880s. The streetscape remains well-preserved to this day. Agents of the city's building department are seen here inspecting the property along with local Chinese residents. (Courtesy of Historic New England; photograph by W. W. K. Campbell.)

QUONG SHUE LUNG COMPANY, 1921. Some of the earliest grocery stores were on Oxford Place and linked with establishments on Harrison Avenue around the corner. Examples include this small grocery store Quong Shue Lung at 2 Oxford Place and the Royal Restaurant at 1 Oxford Place but with a front entrance at 19 Harrison Avenue. No. 3 was a noodle company that survived until the 1930s. All of No. 1 to No. 3 of Oxford Place were demolished later while No. 4 to No. 11 still exist today. (Courtesy of Historic New England; photograph by W. W. K. Campbell.)

TYLER STREET ON THE LEFT, C. 1925. By the 1920s, Tyler Street was well developed into a Chinese commercial district. There was an unbroken string of row houses and buildings occupying almost the whole block between Kneeland and Beach Streets. Stores include two restaurants and two grocery stores on the west side of the street. Store owners and restaurant workers can be seen taking a break from work. (Courtesy of International Society.)

TYLER STREET ON THE RIGHT, C. 1925. The King Wah Low restaurant at No. 12 Tyler Street and the Joy Hong Low restaurant at No. 8 have signage illuminated with light bulbs. The term *chop suey* became a catchphrase for these and other restaurants to appeal to non-Chinese customers. The street was filled with vehicles along restaurant row. An elevated train track is visible along Beach Street. (Courtesy of International Society.)

HUDSON STREET, C. 1925. Hudson Street was mostly occupied by the new Syrian immigrants south of Kneeland Street in the early 20th century, but Chinese began to settle and own businesses along Hudson Street by the 1920s. One store was Hip Yeng Chong Company at 49 Hudson Street. (Courtesy of International Society.)

BEACH STREET NEIGHBORS, 1928. Beach Street served several different ethnic immigrant groups in the 1920s. The elevated train (known as the "El") ran overhead in front of these stores. Weston's Lunch and the Oreig Sewing Machine Company were located east of Hudson Street. Chinese stores were primarily located further west, one block up. (Courtesy of Historic New England.)

BEACH STREET ELEVATED TRAIN STATION, 1941. Between 1899 and 1942, the station of the elevated train was located on Beach Street around the corner from Harrison Avenue. On the left where the American and Chinese flags fly are the Moy Family Association and the Lee Family Association. (Courtesy of Historic New England.)

DEMOLISHING BEACH STREET STATION, 1942. After a train accident occurred in 1938, the City of Boston decided to demolish the aging tracks to accommodate growing automobile traffic. The demolition of train tracks in Chinatown took place in the spring of 1942. Workers can be seen on top of the platform during the elevated train removal. (Courtesy of Historic New England.)

REMOVAL OF THE ELEVATED AT HARRISON AVENUE, 1942. By May 19, 1942, the elevated train had been removed from Beach Street between Harrison Avenue and Tyler Street, while work continued on the tracks east of Hudson Street. At this time, the Beach Street storefronts were occupied by a mixture of Chinese and non-Chinese businesses. (Courtesy of Historic New England.)

BEACH STREET AFTER REMOVAL OF THE ELEVATED, 1942. By June 24, 1942, the entire elevated train track on Beach Street had been removed. Automobiles lined this busy commercial district again and business began to boom, especially after World War II. (Courtesy of Historic New England.)

OLDEST GROCERY STORE SIGN, EARLY 1900S. Among the earliest and longest operating Chinese establishments in Boston was the Quong Wah Lung and Company at 56 Beach Street, from the 1890s to the 1970s. In the early years, grocery stores also served as community information centers or credit unions for overseas remittance transactions. The sign announces the availability of groceries, embroidery and jewelry from Suzhou and Hangzhou, ginseng, medicine, cookware, and antiques. (Courtesy of Frank Chin.)

CHINESE PHARMACY, 1950s. Grocery stores such as Quong Wah Lung also carried many herbal ingredients to fill Chinese medical prescriptions for improving health or curing illness. Here Wei Sun Wong uses a Chinese scale to measure out herbs. (Courtesy of CHSNE collection.)

SELLING TEAS AND GROCERIES, 1930s. Chong Lung Kee at 18 Hudson Street was in business from the 1920s to the 1960s and served the growing Chinese community in those decades. The store sold everything from tea and soap to fish and vegetables. (Courtesy of CHSNE collection.)

OLDEST EXISTING GROCERY STORE, 1950S.
Sun Sun Company, opened by Wong Gow Sue in the 1930s, is the oldest existing grocery store in Chinatown. The store was first on Edinboro Street, at the corner of Beach Street, as seen in this 1950s photograph of Wong, before it moved to two different locations on Oxford Street in the 1960s and 1980s. (Courtesy of David S. Y. Wong.)

INTERIOR OF GROCERY STORE, 1940S. In the early days, store shelves of the groceries were stocked mostly with canned products and bottled sauces, while fresh produce and preserved meats were displayed in baskets in front of a refrigerated case, as can be seen in this interior photograph of the Sun Sun Company in the 1950s. (Courtesy of David S. Y. Wong.)

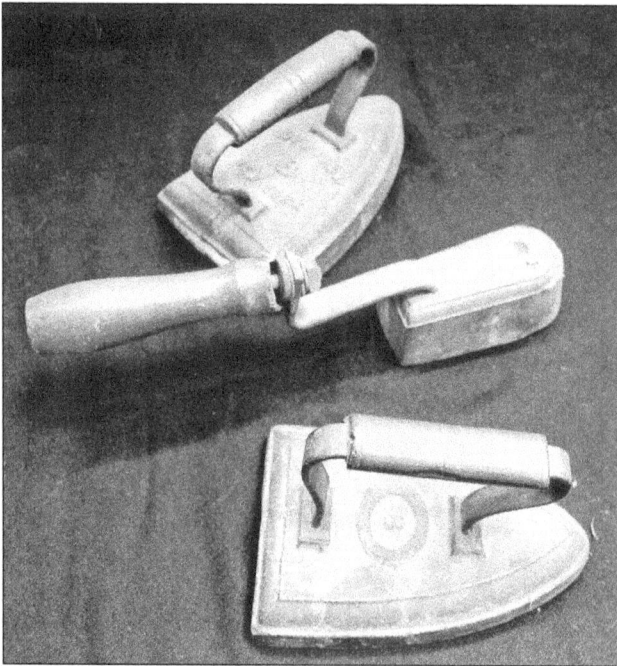

CHINESE LAUNDRY IRONS, EARLY 1900s. Prior to the use of electric irons, Chinese laundry workers heated heavy irons like these on hot coals to press shirts and linens. (Courtesy of CHSNE collection.)

YEE WAH LAUNDRY, 1901. The Boston city directory of 1875 listed three Chinese-owned laundries, but the earliest visual evidence is this photograph showing the front entrance of the Yee Wah Laundry at 59 Beach Street, around the corner from Tyler Street adjacent to an Irish pub. (Courtesy of Historic New England.)

LEE'S LAUNDRY, 1914. By the early 20th century, Chinese laundries were all over the city of Boston and the suburbs. This photograph, dated 1914, shows Lee's laundry on Cambridge Street in the West End of Boston. (Courtesy of International Society.)

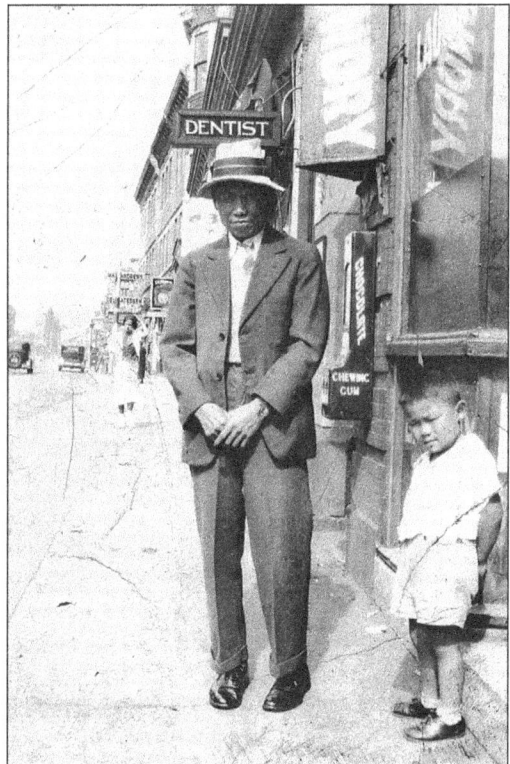

FAMILY LAUNDRY, 1935. Many Chinese-owned laundries were run by entire families. Frank Dong and his wife Susan opened a laundry at 336 Blue Hill Avenue in the Roxbury section of Boston in the early 1930s. Their three-year-old son David and Frank's cousin Yook Gvoon Dong are pictured here in 1935. (Courtesy of Frank and Susan Dong family collection.)

CHILD IN FRONT OF A LAUNDRY, 1935. Many Chinese children who grew up in the 1930s spent their days at family-owned laundries or restaurants when not in school. Some lived at the family-owned business. Here David Dong stands in front of his family's laundry. The family lived on the second and third floors of the laundry until the 1960s. (Courtesy of Frank and Susan Dong family collection.)

INSIDE OF THE LAUNDRY, 1950S. Photographs inside a laundry are rare as most people did not deem such workplaces as worthwhile settings for photographs. This candid shot shows James Dong, son of laundry owner Frank Dong, with his dog in front of the washtub and laundry basket where his mother Susan is hard at work. James has changed into a tuxedo to get ready for his second job at the other family business, a restaurant. (Courtesy of Frank and Susan Dong family collection.)

YEE SING LAUNDRY IN CONCORD, 1930S. After a heavy snow storm on an early March day, a young Chinese laundry worker clears snow from the front of a laundry in Concord. (Courtesy of Concord Free Public Library.)

READY TO SERVE THE NEXT CUSTOMER, 1976. In this photograph, little Yee has climbed up on to the makeshift reception desk alongside a huge stack of hand-wrapped laundry packages, awaiting the next customer. This photograph, taken in the 1970s, represents the tail end of the era of the Chinese-owned laundry business. (Courtesy of Boston Globe; photograph by Stan Grossfeld.)

WORK AND PLAY IN FAMILY LAUNDRY, 1976. While both parents operated the family business, the laundry had to serve as a "playground" for children, such as 2-year-old little Yee, seen here hiding inside a laundry cart at the Charlie Loy Laundry in Brighton. (Courtesy of Boston Globe; photograph by Stan Grossfeld.)

HONG FAR LOW RESTAURANT, 1920S. As the earliest Chinatown restaurant, the Hong Far Low on Harrison Avenue was still in business after several decades, serving chop suey and lunch specials for 35¢ in the 1920s. The Chinese American Citizens Alliance was now established and located upstairs at 34 Harrison Avenue next door. A pharmacy owned by a Caucasian affectionately known as "Uncle Seth" is also next door, with its bilingual signs to attract both non-Chinese and Chinese customers. (Courtesy of Dorothy Wong.)

HONG FAR LOW

First Class Chinese Restaurant with private booths

34½, 36½, 38½ Harrison Ave., Boston, Mass.
Telephone Hancock 7016

ADVERTISEMENT OF RESTAURANTS, 1931. The Chinese Directory of New England, published in 1931, contained advertisements as well as listings of restaurants. Hong Far Low tried to promote its image as a first-class Chinese restaurant with an advertisement showcasing private booths. Its advertisement mixes an image of traditional appeal, that of a Chinese female, with modern service in the Western style. (Courtesy of CHSNE collection.)

TONG WAR AND SI WOO RESTAURANT, 1923. In addition to glamour, the 1920s was also characterized by the lingering conflicts between the Hip Sing Tong and the On Leong Tong dating back to the late 1800s. A newspaper publication created this image of a murder scene for insertion over the photograph of the Si Woo restaurant at 22 Harrison Avenue. By 1931, the restaurant had closed. (Courtesy of International Society.)

JOY HONG LOW RESTAURANT AND GOON FAMILY ASSOCIATION, 1929.
At 8 and 10 Tyler Street stood two of the most spectacular buildings in the 1920s. The Joy Hong Low restaurant was opened around 1920 with a large chop suey sign and later remodeled with traditional Chinese motifs. The Goon Family Association purchased 10 Tyler Street with its second-story balcony and third-story facade around 1927 to house a new family association. The Boston Landmarks Commission considered this building as the "most elaborate example of traditional Chinese urban architecture in Boston" and a "landmark of Chinatown development" in a 1990s report. (Courtesy of Historic New England.)

TWO TYPICAL CHINESE RESTAURANTS, 1925.
Hon Hong Low and Ngar Hong Guey were two restaurants with Toishanese names located at 25 and 21 Tyler Street, respectively. Tyler Street had become the leading restaurant district of Chinatown before the Second World War. (Courtesy of CHSNE collection.)

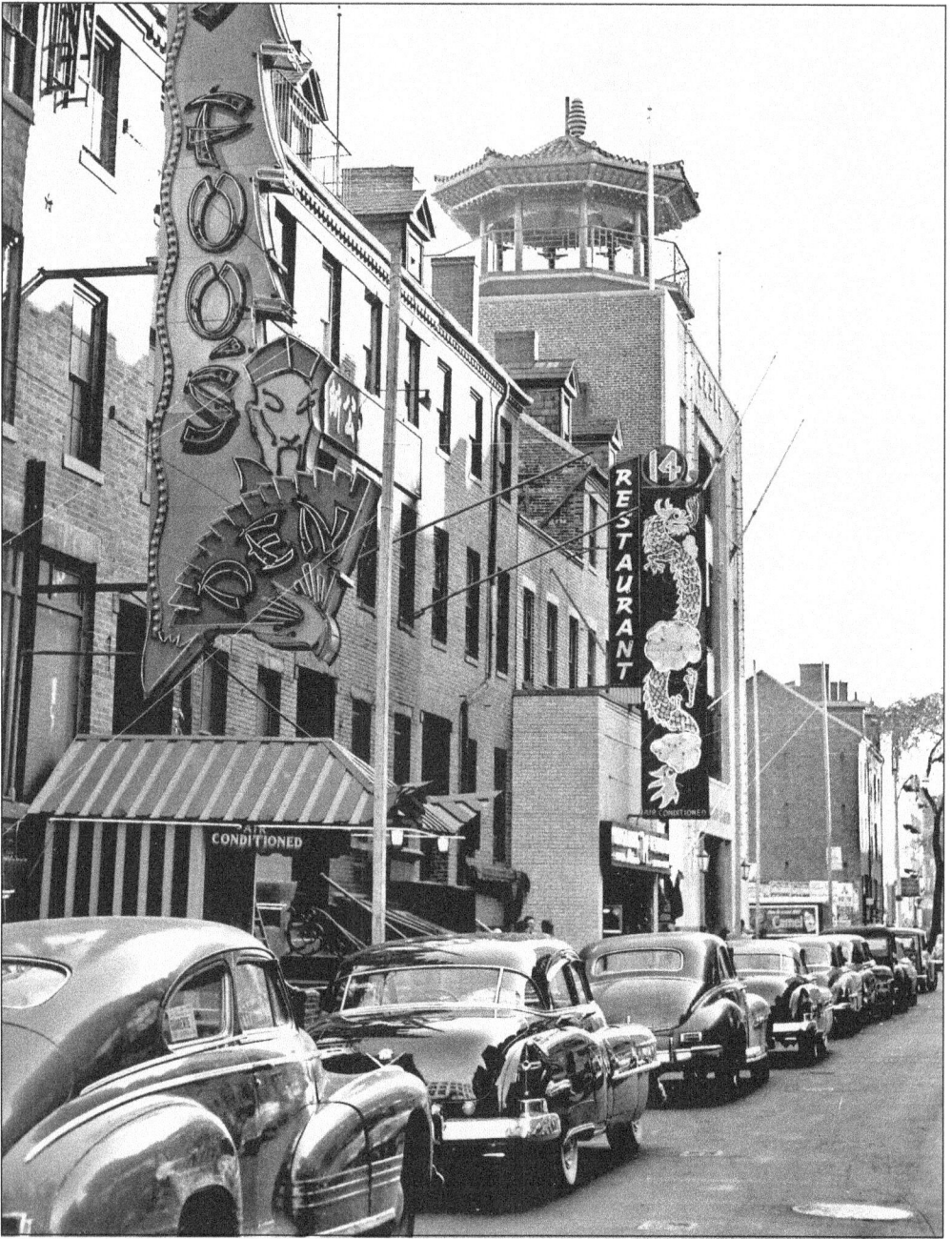

RUBY FOO'S DEN, 1951. Ruby Foo's Den at 6 Hudson Street was opened in 1929. The owner Ruby Foo was one of the earliest Chinese female restaurant owners in the country. Her restaurant successfully catered to non-Chinese and a celebrity clientele. It was the most famous restaurant for non-Chinese customers in the 1930s. Note the number of cars parked outside. (Courtesy of CHSNE collection.)

CHINATOWN'S "SMARTEST RESTAURANT." The menu cover of Ruby Foo's Den marketed itself as Chinatown's "smartest restaurant." The decor was artistic and it appealed to elite customers. (Courtesy of CHSNE collection.)

Boston's Most Unusual Eating Place
THE GOOD EARTH

BOSTON'S MOST UNUSUAL EATING PLACE. The Good Earth restaurant was another famous restaurant with an anglicized name that was opened in the 1930s. The decor was more westernized and was one of the first restaurants with air-conditioned rooms. It advertised itself as Boston's most unusual eating place. (Courtesy of CHSNE collection.)

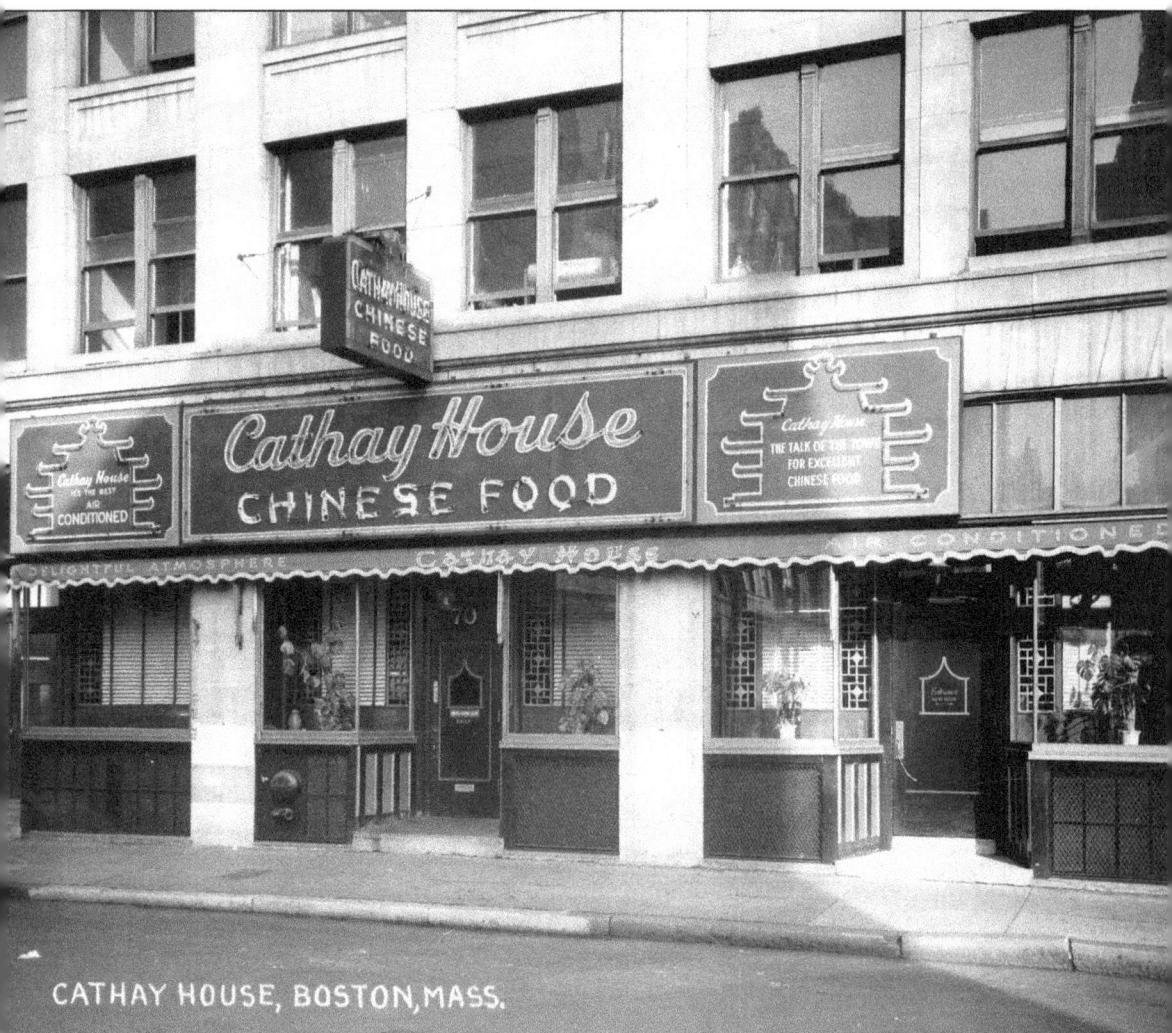

CATHAY HOUSE, BOSTON, MASS.

CATHAY HOUSE RESTAURANT, 1946. Cathay House at 70 Beach Street was opened around 1940 by Gordon and Anita Chue. This photograph shows the outside of the restaurant in 1946, with its sign hawking a delightful atmosphere and air-conditioned comfort. It also advertised itself as the talk of the town for excellent Chinese food. (Courtesy of Bostonian Society.)

No. 9 Tyler Street, 1955.
Restaurants with Chinese names were difficult for non-Chinese patrons to pronounce and remember, so many restaurants resorted to the use of their street numbers in signage or as part of their English name to help. The Hon Loy Doo restaurant was better known as "the No. 9" outside the Chinatown community. It opened in 1951 and had a dance hall serving Chinese American food. (Courtesy of Rotch Visual Collection, MIT library; photograph by Nishan Bichajian.)

Banquet for Chinese Ambassador, 1957. Hon Loy Doo restaurant eventually adopted an English name, China Pearl, and reduced the size of the numeral 9 in its signage. It is one of the leading places for dim sum in the city. In 1957, Chinatown leaders were in full force welcoming the visit of the Chinese ambassador to the second floor of the restaurant. (Courtesy of Bill Chin.)

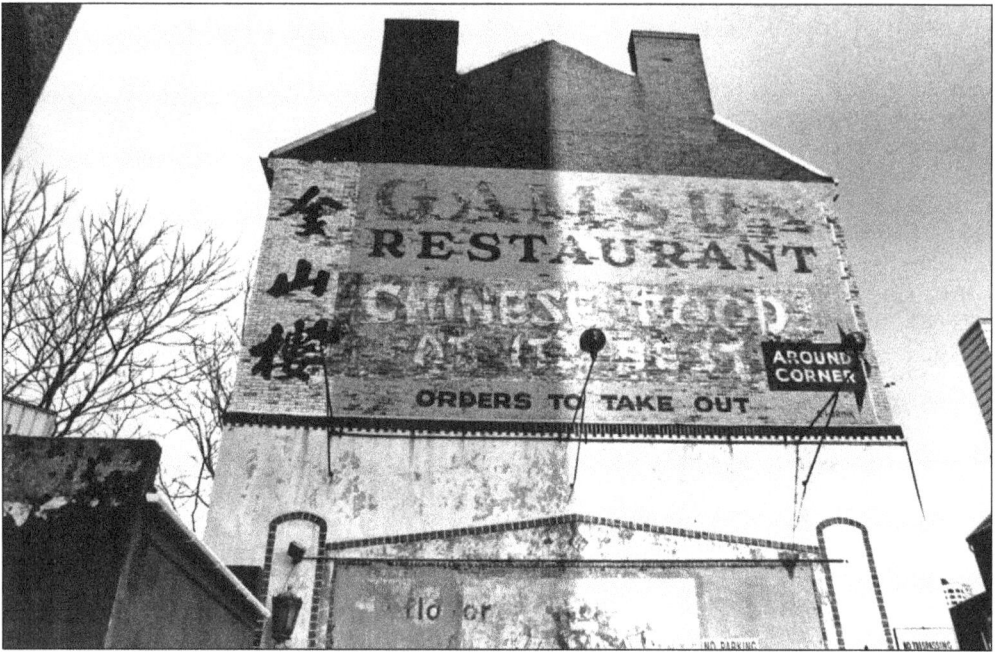

SIGN OF GAMSUN RESTAURANT, 1960S. Gamsun ("gold mountain") restaurant, at 21 Hudson Street, was another popular restaurant in the 1940s and 1950s. The restaurant was sold to make way for the Shanghai Restaurant during the 1960s, but its painted brick billboard remains today on Kneeland Street as a reminder of the past. (Courtesy of CHSNE collection.)

EASTERN LIVE POULTRY STORE, 1970S. Joseph Berman's Eastern Live Poultry Shop at 48 Beach Street catered to the community's desire for freshly killed poultry for 91 years. It was purchased by a Chinese American family a few years ago. (Courtesy of CHSNE collection.)

Three

COMMUNITY, CULTURE, AND EDUCATION

CHINESE JUNIOR HIGH SCHOOL BAND, 1944. The Quong (Kwong) Kow Chinese School was founded by the Chinese Merchants Association in 1916. The school organized a junior high school band that was active in the 1930s and 1940s. Band members were photographed here with school staff and community leaders outside the vice consulate office in Boston on March 1, 1944. (Courtesy of CHSNE collection.)

TERCENTENARY PARADE IN BOSTON, 1930. Youth from the Chinese community marched and posed along Boylston Street holding flags of both the United States and the Republic of China on the occasion of the 300th birthday of the City of Boston. This picture is featured in the 1931 Chinese Directory of New England. (Courtesy of CHSNE collection.)

波 城 各 團 體

CHINESE CLUBS AND ASSOCIATIONS OF BOSTON

中 華 公 所	United Chinese Association	14 Oxford St.
致 公 堂	Chinese Free Mason	6 Tyler St.
安良工商會	Chinese Merchants Association	2 Tyler St.
華人青年會	Chinese Y. M. C. A.	56 Tyler St.
國 民 黨	Kuo Min Tang	17 Hudson St.
黃江夏堂	Wong Gong Har Hong	10 Hudson St.
雲山公所	Wong Won Sun Associatio.	10 Hudson St.
余武溪公所	Yee Moo Kai Association	23 Hudson St.
龍岡公所	Lung Quong Association	15 Tyler St.
至 德 堂	Coo Duck Association	52 Tyler St.

LISTING OF FAMILY AND COMMUNITY ASSOCIATIONS, 1931. The Chinese Directory of New England was published by the Hop Yuen Company at 16 Oxford Street in May 1931. The company was subsequently bought by Henry Y. M. Wong and changed its name to the Shanghai Printing Company in 1932. The directory provided a listing of Chinese clubs, family associations, restaurants, and laundries in Greater Boston in 1931. Feature articles described a tremendous growth of community culture in the 1920s. The printing business is currently run by Wong's son Jeffrey. (Courtesy of CHSNE collection.)

MEMORIAL SERVICE FOR DR. SUN YAT-SEN IN BOSTON, 1925. Chinese revolutionary leader Dr. Sun Yat-sen gained widespread support from overseas Chinese in overthrowing the Qing dynasty in 1911. Chinese Nationalist Party branches were subsequently established in major American cities including Boston. The Boston branch was founded at 10 Hudson Street before it was relocated to 17 Hudson Street. Dr. Sun died of cancer during the Northern Expedition on March 12, 1925. Photographed is a group of Chinese Nationalist Party members in Boston in a solemn memorial ceremony one month after the death of Dr. Sun outside the party branch office. (Courtesy of Frank and Kay Chin.)

THE CHINESE NATIONALIST PARTY BRANCH, 1967. The Chinese Nationalist Party (Kuo Min Tang) headquarters in Boston was located at 17 Hudson Street. It actively supported local community associations for many decades, especially after the Chinese Communist Party took power in China in 1949. This photograph shows the apex of the organization in Chinatown in 1967. (Courtesy of Cynthia Yee.)

DELEGATES OF CHINESE NATIONALIST PARTY MEETING, 1967. A portrait of Dr. Sun Yat-sen, founder of the Republic of China, hung in the hall where the delegates of the Chinese Nationalist Party in Boston met in the 1960s. (Courtesy of Cynthia Yee.)

CHINESE MERCHANTS ASSOCIATION, C. 1943. The Chinese Merchants Association set up its headquarters at 2 Tyler Street from 1919 to 1951 before moving to 20 Hudson Street. The organization was first founded in Boston around 1914 to promote unity and provide support among Chinese merchants in Boston. Bunting was hung outside the building in celebration of the 39th annual national convention held in Boston around 1943. (Courtesy of International Society.)

TRADITIONAL CHINESE BALCONY, C. 1943. A close-up view of the Chinese Merchants Association shows the facade remodeled with a traditional Chinese balcony as a landmark of Boston Chinatown. Wah Luck Guey restaurant was on the corner at Beach Street. (Courtesy of International Society.)

CHINESE MERCHANT, 1920S. This portrait, in oil, of Y. Chin was painted in the 1920s. Chin was an early Chinatown merchant who was successful in opening an herbal store and who returned several times to China. He died in Boston in 1934. He had eight children, several of whom returned to Boston to become important civic leaders in Chinatown starting in the 1960s. (Courtesy of Bill and Frank Chin.)

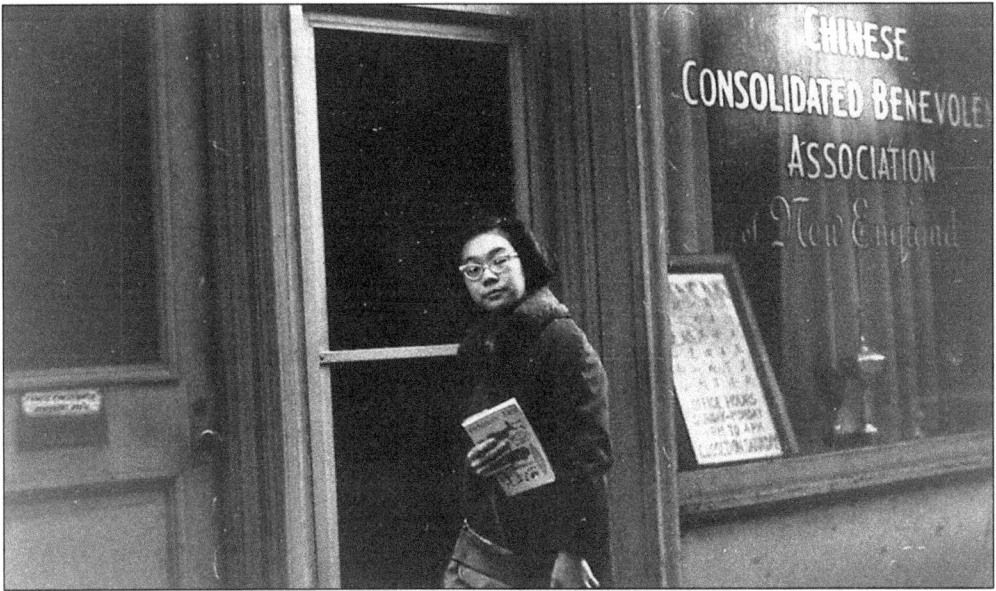

CHINESE CONSOLIDATED BENEVOLENT ASSOCIATION OF NEW ENGLAND, 1950S. The Chinese Consolidated Benevolent Association of New England, known as the CCBA, was the umbrella organization for different community and business organizations. It was founded in the second decade of the 20th century after similar headquarters were established in San Francisco and New York. From the 1920s to the 1970s, the office was located at 14 Oxford Street, as seen here, before moving to 90 Tyler Street. (Courtesy of Stephanie Fan.)

MOY FAMILY ASSOCIATION BUILDING, 1955. The Moy Family Association was formed by one of the earliest Toishanese immigrant families in Boston at the beginning of the 20th century. Established in the 1930s, it was first located at 52 Beach Street, and then relocated to Hudson Street. (Courtesy of Rotch Visual Collection, MIT library; photograph by Nishan Bichajian.)

YEE FAMILY ASSOCIATION ALTAR, 1927. Family shrines served as the focus of clan activities during annual festivals and ancestral rites. By the 1920s, public street rituals were mostly replaced by ancestral worship inside the family associations. The family association members presented chicken, fruit, and other offerings to the ancestors in annual celebrations. The family shrine at the Yee Family Association at 23 Hudson Street is shown here in a photograph taken in February 1927. (Courtesy of International Society.)

WONG FAMILY ASSOCIATION BUILDING, 1950s. The Wong name is one of the major surnames among early settlers in Boston Chinatown. The Wong Family Association was founded in the 1920s and was located at 10 Hudson Street before it moved to Beach Street in its current location. (Courtesy of CHSNE collection.)

GEE HOW OAK TIN ASSOCIATION BUILDING, 1964. The Gee How Oak Tin Association was first founded in San Francisco in 1920. The Boston branch opened a year after the formation of the local Chin Family Association. It organized the fifth national convention in 1929. In 1964, it moved to its present site on the second floor of 77 Harrison Avenue after purchasing the building in 1960. (Courtesy of Peter Chan.)

LEADERS OF GEE HOW OAK TIN ASSOCIATION, 1964. The 1960s were a transitional period for the family associations as the post–World War II younger generation began to assume more important roles in the organizations. The youthful faces of the leadership at Gee How Oak Tin Association in 1964 were indicative of this new trend. (Courtesy of Peter Chan.)

63

OPENING CEREMONY OF NEW BUILDING, 1964. The celebration of the grand opening of the Gee How Oak Tin Association at 77 Harrison Avenue included hundreds of family members. The association is dominated by the Chins, but it also includes those with the surnames of Woo and Yuen. (Courtesy of Bill Chin and Gee How Oak Tin Association.)

LEE FAMILY ASSOCIATION BUILDING, 1970S. The Lee Family Association was founded in the 1920s, and was at 50 Beach Street until it purchased the building at 10 Tyler Street from the Goon Family Association. This building maintains one of the grandest traditional Chinese balconies in the Chinatown area. (Courtesy of CHSNE collection.)

CELEBRATION OF LEE FAMILY ASSOCIATION, 1960. Leaders and members of the Lee Family Association celebrated the opening day of the newly purchased building with festivities continuing into the evening. (Courtesy of Lee Family Association.)

十
月九民
四年國 念紀影撮賓來暨表代禮典幕開遷喬成落所公氏李僑□

OPENING OF LEE FAMILY ASSOCIATION BUILDING, 1960. After purchasing the building, the Lee Family Association occupied three floors for its member activities. They later made one of the floors exclusively for Lee family women to set up a ladies' auxiliary. This photograph captures the grand celebration of the opening of the Lee Family Association on October 16, 1960. This day is now celebrated every year with a grand banquet. (Courtesy of Lee Family Association.)

YEE FUNG TOY ASSOCIATION, 1970S. Originally named the Yee Moo Kai Association, the Yee Fung Toy association promotes solidarity among the Yee family members. It holds regular meetings and was a place for Yee bachelors to seek support and to network upon and following their arrival in the region. (Courtesy of International Society.)

KEW SING MUSIC CLUB, 1951. This music society was founded in 1939 by eight amateur musicians to promote and preserve Chinese traditional music and Cantonese opera in New England. The club performed in a concert at the new building of the Chinese Merchant Association on Hudson Street in 1951 on the occasion of the building dedication. (Courtesy of CHSNE collection.)

CHINESE OPERA PERFORMERS AND MUSICIANS, 1965. Kew Sing Music Club frequently hosted visiting opera troupes and performers in the 1950s and the 1960s. Club members practiced traditional Chinese music instruments and the opera singing style with occasional performances in full costume. The visiting opera troupe photographed here performed with Kew Sing club members in 1965. (Courtesy of CHSNE collection.)

BULLETIN BOARD ON OXFORD STREET, 1941. Aside from an early attempt in the 1890s to publish a newspaper, the fastest and most effective way to spread the news was through the community bulletin board constructed on the wall of the building at the corner of Oxford and Beach Streets. It displayed announcements, job notices, news items, and cultural events for the early settlers and bachelors in Chinatown. The bulletin board, which was divided into sections for different organizations, served as the primary means of communication until the 1970s. (Courtesy of International Society.)

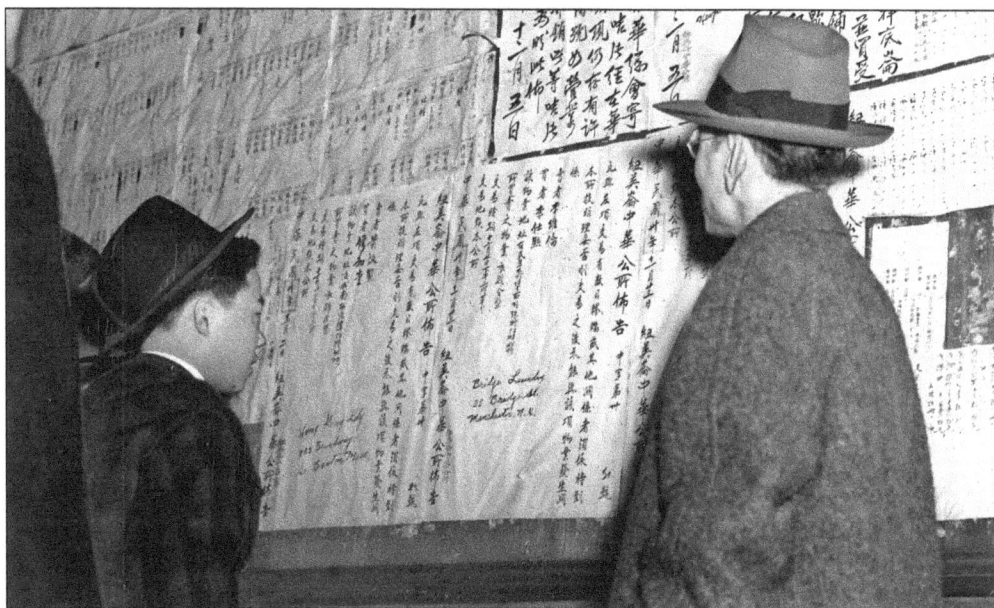

BULLETIN BOARD AND WARTIME NEWS, 1940S. During World War II, events in China provoked strong interest among Chinese residents in Boston. The bulletin board helped to foster community cohesiveness and served as a neighborhood resource center. It also helped residents to learn about events in China during the turbulent years before, during, and after World War II. (Courtesy of CHSNE collection.)

FEMALE AUDIENCE OF THE BULLETIN BOARD, 1957. After the Second World War, the number of women and families began to grow. In this photograph, four young ladies, Elizabeth Jung, Lan Lee, Shirley Soohoo, and Lillian Ming, read news about the Chinese Christian Church. Unable to compete with Chinese language newspapers, the bulletin board finally came down in 1991. (Courtesy of Boston Herald-Traveler and CHSNE collection.)

SHANGHAI PRINTING COMPANY, 1956. In 1932, Henry Wong opened the Shanghai Printing Company after buying the business from the Hop Yuen Company on Oxford Street. Typesetting, prior to the use of Chinese typewriters and word processors, required the memorization of the placement of thousands of Chinese characters along these wall cases. Most of the print jobs were for Chinese restaurant menus and laundry tickets. (Courtesy of Wong family.)

HARVARD CHINESE STUDENTS CLUB

表生學國中佛大哈

DIRECTORY (1930-1931)

張心源	Chang, H. Y.	(Kiangsu), Law 60 Walker St., Cambridge
幸伯堪	Chang, Sherman J. K.	(Chekiang), Fellow in Law 61 Garfield St., Cambridge
張友熙	Chang, Sherman Y.	(Hupeh), Radio 65 Hammond St., Cambridge
張 維	Chang, W.	(Honan), Public Health 68 Francis St., Boston
趙韻熊	Chao, C. H.	(Kiangsu), Literature 55 Ellery St., Cambridge
趙訪熊	Chao, Robert F. H.	(Kiangsu), Mathematics 27 Trowbridge St., Cambridge
陳心陶	Chen, H. T.	(Fukien), Parasitology Vanderbilt 444, Boston
陳 嘉	Chen, Karl C.	(Chekiang), Literature 351 Harvard St., Cambridge
陳麟瑞	Chen, L. J.	(Chekiang), Literature 21 Trowbridge St., Cambridge
陳志潛	Chen, C. C.	(Szechuen), Public Health 68 Francis St., Boston
祁佛智	Chi, K. T.	(Hupeh), Physics 16 Wendell St., Cambridge
江啓泰	Chiang, C. T.	(Fukien), Government 351 Harvard St., Cambridge
喬文壽	Chiao, W. S.	(Kiangsu), Banking 3 Chauncy St., Cambridge
朱珍珊	Chiao, W. S., Mrs.	(Kiangsu), Biology, Radcliffe 3 Chauncy St., Cambridge
喬志千	Chiao, C. C.	(Shensi), Business 5 Putnam Avenue, Cambridge
錢乃信	Chien, N. H.	(Kwangtung), Law 29 Wendell St., Cambridge
陳福田	Ching, F. T.	(Hawaii), Literature. Professor (Tsing Haa) 9 Wendell St., Cambridge
朱人熙	Chu, H. J.	(Kiangsu), Geology 57 Gorham St., Cambridge
周 田	Chow, Bacon F.	(Fukien), Chemistry 351 Harvard St., Cambridge
戴葆銓	Dai, B. C.	(Kwangtung), Government 19 Trowbridge St., Cambridge
杜細洲	Doo, S. C.	(Kwangtung), Law 26 Mellen St., Cambridge
范存忠	Fan, T. C.	(Kiangsu), Literature 25 Trowbridge St., Cambridge
方頤績	Fang, I. C.	(Kiangsu), Public Health 68 Francis St., Boston
赫英舉	He, Y. C.	(Liaoning), Sanitary Engineering 40 Francis St., Boston
何 麟	Ho, Philip L.	(Kwangtung), Business McCulloch C-39, Soldiers Field Boston
謝佐禹	Hsieh, T. Y.	(Kwangtung), Philosophy Harvard St., Cambridge
胡敦元	Hu, T. Y.	(Anhwei), Economics 1118 Massachusetts Ave.

LISTING OF CHINESE STUDENTS AT HARVARD, 1931. Chinese students from Harvard University founded their first student organization in 1917. It became a matter of local pride for the Chinese Directory of New England in 1931 to print the names of Chinese students attending university at Harvard and MIT. (Courtesy of CHSNE collection.)

PRINCIPAL OF QUONG KOW CHINESE SCHOOL, 1934. One of the students who studied for a master's degree at Harvard was T. S. Tse, who came from Lingnan University in Guangzhou. Tse and another student at Harvard became principals of Quong Kow (later known as Kwong Kow) Chinese School in Chinatown in the early and mid-1930s. (Courtesy of CHSNE collection.)

廣 教 校 刊

中華民國二十三年九月

第 一 卷 第 一 號

美國波士頓廣教初級中學印行

The Quong Kow Journal

PUBLISHED BY

QUONG KOW CHINESE SCHOOL

20 OXFORD STREET

BOSTON, MASS. U.S.A.

VOLUME 1   NUMBER 1   SEPTEMBER 1934

QUONG KOW CHINESE SCHOOL JOURNAL, 1934. Scholar T. S. Tse contributed articles to the 1931 Chinese Directory of New England. He also helped to publish the first Quong Kow school journal, the cover of which is seen here. The journal contains many essays from teachers and students of the school. (Courtesy of CHSNE collection.)

The First Commence
Boston Mass. June

CHINESE SCHOOL GRADUATION CEREMONY, 1931. This extraordinarily detailed photograph presents a comprehensive portrait of the students and faculty during the graduation ceremony of the Quong Kow Chinese School at 18 Oxford Street in 1931. The school was founded by the

Chinese Merchants Association in 1916 to promote Chinese language and heritage. The large number of children indicates that there was a remarkable growth in the number of Chinese families in the 1920s. (Courtesy of CHSNE collection.)

CHINESE SCHOOL BAND, 1940. The Quong Kow Chinese School organized a very active junior high school band that performed regularly in Chinatown in the 1930s and 1940s. Most of the band members were boys; the few participating girls played the role of drum majorettes. (Courtesy of Mary Soo Hoo.)

CHINESE SCHOOL GRADUATION DIPLOMA, 1942. The Chinese school awarded diplomas to graduates of both the sixth and the ninth grades. This sixth grade diploma was presented to Tunney Lee. (Courtesy of Tunney Lee.)

CHINESE SCHOOL GRADUATION CLASS PHOTOGRAPH, 1949. This graduation photograph provokes the question of whether there were more females than boys or whether the girls were more persistent in earning a diploma. (Courtesy of Josephine Chin.)

FEMALE DRUM MAJORETTE, 1946. After the Second World War the Quong Kow junior high school band occasionally performed for returning soldiers. Josephine Chin was the drum majorette in the high school band and is shown here marching on the streets of Boston for a victory parade. (Courtesy of Josephine Chin.)

INSIDE THE CHINESE CLASSROOM, C. 1950. Randy Tow and other students in the classroom of the Quong Kow school listened to principal Loy Wong's instructions about the procedure for an awards ceremony. (Courtesy of Reggie Wong.)

QUINCY SCHOOL, C. 1902–1904.
The Quincy School was
established in 1847 at 90 Tyler
Street. It was regarded as the
first school in the country with
graded classrooms and the first to
provide a separate seat for each
student. There were almost no
Chinese students in the early
days. Students in this picture
were mostly of Syrian descent.
The front of the original building
is shown here with four stories,
before a powerful hurricane
destroyed the top floor in 1938.
(Courtesy of Boston Athenaeum.)

QUINCY SCHOOL, 1962. By the early
1960s, the Chinese had replaced the
Syrians as the largest ethnic group
at the Quincy School. In 1976, the
aging school structure was sold by
the city to the Chinese Consolidated
Benevolent Association for
community programming and
the Quincy School itself moved
into a brand new facility at
885 Washington Street with its full
name, the Josiah Quincy School.
(Courtesy of International Society.)

77

QUINCY SCHOOL CLASS PHOTOGRAPH, 1942. This third-grade class photograph during World War II shows that Chinese students constituted only about 20 percent of the class at that time. The majority of students in the 1940s were Syrian immigrant children. (Courtesy of Alice Hom.)

QUINCY SCHOOL CLASS PHOTOGRAPH, 1950s. This class photograph shows the diverse racial and ethnic composition of the students in Quincy School in the 1950s. (Courtesy of CHSNE collection.)

QUINCY SCHOOL READING HOUR, 1946. Chinese American children spent more time reading English books than studying Chinese during the 1940s. Six-year-old Sherry Chue reads *Flip* to a very attentive five-year-old Caroline Wong at Quincy School in 1946. (Courtesy of International Society.)

CHINESE NEW YEAR HOLIDAY IN QUINCY SCHOOL, 1946. Chinese children of the Quincy School on Tyler Street, gathered in a classroom after World War II with a ceremonial lion for the first peaceful New Year in many years. (Courtesy of International Society.)

CHINESE BOY SCOUTS, C. 1930. The Chinese Americans Citizens League at 36 Harrison Avenue sponsored Troop 34 of the Boy Scouts in the early 1930s. Roger Duncan, the assistant scoutmaster, is at the back in the center of the picture. The scoutmaster was Moy Yee Sing, not pictured. Many of these children were the first generation in Chinatown to receive an education from kindergarten through high school in Boston's public schools. (Courtesy of Boston Herald-Traveler and CHSNE collection.)

CHILD ON HUDSON STREET, LATE 1940S. David Gin Woo races along Hudson Street in the late 1940s. The south end of Hudson Street was a street in Chinatown with mostly Chinese, Syrian, and Lebanese residents. It possessed such a strong sense of community that, decades after highway land-taking displaced most of the local residents, the loss of community is still mourned. (Courtesy of Reggie Wong.)

Four

WOMEN, FAMILIES, AND ACTIVISM

CHINESE GIRLS AT DENISON SETTLEMENT HOUSE, C. 1930. Chinese girls formed their own basketball team at the Denison Settlement House on Tyler Street, around 1930. Founded in 1892 by the College Settlement House Association, Denison House, a woman-run settlement house, occupied three adjoining buildings for 50 years until the end of World War II. Their shop sold crafts produced by local women. They ran a medical dispensary, a milk station, and taught English. Chinese women were served along with Lebanese, Syrian, and Italian immigrant women. (Courtesy of Schlesinger Library, Radcliffe Institute, Harvard University.)

TWO YOUNG WOMEN IN CHINA, EARLY 1930S. Most of the earliest Chinese female residents of Boston arrived when Chinese workers returned to China to marry, usually by family arrangement, or to bring along a wife who had stayed behind while he worked in America. These two young women are from the Wong family and came to Boston in the 1930s and 1940s. (Courtesy of Reggie Wong.)

WOMAN AND CHILDREN IN PHOTO STUDIO, 1923. Many women who came to Boston in the 1920s and 1930s arranged for studio or professional portraits since few, if any, had personal cameras. Undoubtedly, a fair number of these photographs were sent back to families in China. Here Mrs. Fuke Wah Chin poses with her two children in 1923 Boston. (Courtesy of Stephanie Fan.)

Two Girls in a Park, 1929. Chinese girls who grew up in Boston in the 1920s had to negotiate between their traditional family customs and modern American life. These two Chinese girls chose to dress in traditional Chinese costumes and enjoyed a leisure outing in a park in 1929. (Courtesy of Schlesinger Library, Radcliffe Institute, Harvard University.)

Girl's Basketball Team and Coach, 1931. Margaret C. Stewart, one of the workers in the Denison House, was the coach of the Denison House Chinese girls' basketball team. Here she poses with a group of Chinese girls who could be the first Chinese female basketball team in Boston. (Courtesy of Schlesinger Library, Radcliffe Institute, Harvard University.)

GIRLS CLEANING CABIN, 1937. The Denison House sometimes organized outdoor activities such as camping in towns outside Boston. The counselor and a group of Chinese girls were photographed at a camp in Georgetown cleaning their cabin in 1937. (Courtesy of Schlesinger Library, Radcliffe Institute, Harvard University.)

FIRST WOMEN LION DANCE TROUPE, 1938. Boston's first women's lion dance troupe was organized to participate in fund-raising from the Chinese community to assist China in its defense during the Sino-Japanese War. The entire troupe consisted of eight girls, most of whom were only 11–12 years old. The march portrayed here took place on July 7, 1938, in memory of the one-year anniversary of Japanese invasion of China. (Courtesy of Hing Soo Hoo and CHSNE collection.)

MARCH OF THE WOMEN'S LION DANCE TROUPE, 1938. Many associations organized activities to raise funds to send to China. Among the activities were weekly lion dance parades, similar to today's "choy chang" performance with the lion head visiting store to store during the Chinese New Year. Every weekend the first Women's Lion Dance troupe would parade through the streets of Boston Chinatown soliciting donations from the businesses. (Courtesy of Hing Soo Hoo and CHSNE collection.)

CHINESE WOMEN TAKE ON LEADERSHIP ROLES, 1940. The role of the women who came to New England began to change dramatically from that of those they left behind in China. At the urging of Madame Chiang, they formed their own association, the New England Chinese Women's New Life Movement. In the process they developed leadership skills and found some degree of independence. The organization was later renamed as the New England Chinese Women's Association. (Courtesy of New England Chinese Women's Association and CHSNE collection.)

CHINESE WOMEN'S NEW LIFE MOVEMENT ASSOCIATION, 1940. Members of the New England Chinese Women's New Life Movement Association gathered together in their Boston Chinatown headquarters on September 1, 1940. The New Life Movement stressed four virtues, propriety, righteousness, honesty, and honor as the principles of life. (Courtesy of International Society; photograph by Fay Foto.)

WOMEN RAISING CHINESE AND AMERICAN FLAGS, 1942. News of the Japanese invasion of China and the American declaration of war after Pearl Harbor had a profound effect on the community. Chinese women lost no time getting involved in street demonstrations, marching with both Chinese and American flags. (Courtesy of CHSNE collection.)

WOMEN RAISING FUNDS FOR WAR EFFORT, 1940S. Women took an active role in raising funds from Chinatown residents to support China during the Sino-Japanese War. (Courtesy of International Society.)

WOMEN ACTIVE IN OPENING OF CHINESE MERCHANTS ASSOCIATION BUILDING, 1951. Helen Chin played an important role in the opening ceremonies for the Chinese Merchants Association when its new building was constructed in 1951. She represents a generation of women that was active in civic organizations organized by both Chinatown and the mainstream American society. (Courtesy of Helen Chin Schlichte.)

THE CHINESE PATRIOTIC FLYING CORPS, 1930S. The Chinese Patriotic Flying Corps was formed in the early 1930s to assist China in its defense against Japanese aggression. The pilots were all trained at East Boston Airport under F. Kendall. The flier in the center of the photograph is 20-year-old Rose Lok. (Courtesy of Layne Wong and CHSNE collection.)

WOMAN AND AVIATION, 1932. Rose Lok was only 18 when she took up flying and joined the Chinese Patriotic Flying Corps in 1932, highly unusual behavior for a young Chinese woman. Lok may well have been inspired by Amelia Earhart, who was working nearby at the Denison Settlement House on Tyler Street during that time, but who also took the time to occasionally fly over the city dropping flyers about the settlement house. (Courtesy of Layne Wong and CHSNE Collection.)

THE ATLANTIC INSTITUTE OF AERONAUTICS

14 OXFORD STREET   BOSTON, MASS.

GROUND SCHOOL DIVISION   NO. 257

AVIATION GROUND SCHOOL CERTIFICATE

To Whom It May Concern:

THIS IS TO CERTIFY THAT   Miss Rose Lok

has completed in the Atlantic Aviation School Ground School Course the work outlined below, and is entitled to credit for number of hours, and for the grade indicated for each course.

All work has been carried on in accordance with the requirements of the United State Department of commerce.

AIR NAVIGATION. 25. hours with a grade of .85. per cent
METEOROLOGY.. 25. hours with a grade of .96. per cent
MILITARY FLYING. ---. hours with a grade of . ---. per cent
RADIO. ---. hours with a grade of . ---. per cent
TOTAL GROUND SCHOOL HOURS . 50.....
ISSUED THIS. 5th DAY OF ...April.... 1934 AT BOSTON, MASS.

WOMAN'S AVIATION CERTIFICATE, 1934. Rose Lok was the first female Chinese American pilot in New England. She received an aviation ground school certificate issued in April 1934. (Courtesy of Layne Wong and CHSNE collection.)

ROSE LOK IN COMMERCIAL, 1950S. Because of her fame and popularity, Lok was recruited for a commercial photograph to promote a pre-packaged chow mein dinner. (Courtesy of Layne Wong and CHSNE collection.)

AMERICAN MOTHER OF THE YEAR, 1952. Born in Guangzhou, China, Toy Len Goon arrived in Portland, Maine, in 1922. She ran a hand laundry there from 1921 to 1952 and raised her eight children single-handedly after her husband's premature death. Her accomplishment earned her the titles of Maine Mother of the Year and American Mother of the Year in 1952. (Courtesy of Edward and Amy Guen and Maine Historical Society.)

TOY LEN GOON IN HER OWN LAUNDRY, 1940S. Toy Len Goon was the owner of Woodfords Corner Laundry in Woodfords, Maine. She is seen here operating equipment used to wring water from laundry. (Courtesy of Doris Wong and Maine Historical Society.)

TOY LEN GOON HONORED BY CHINATOWN PARADE, 1952. Goon was welcomed to New York in a Chinatown parade on May 10, 1952. Traditional lion dances were featured in the procession through the narrow streets of the Chinese American community. In the back seat with Goon is Shing Tai Liang, a local leader. (Courtesy of Doris Wong and Maine Historical Society, United Press photograph.)

MARYKNOLL SISTERS CENTER, 1953.
The Maryknoll Sisters Center was a
Catholic charitable organization that
served the Chinatown community
from 1946 to 1992. Rose Chin and
Anne Wong are seen here distributing
leaflets to Emily Yee and June Wong
announcing the free chest X-ray
survey to be conducted in Chinatown
in September 1953. (Courtesy of
the Boston Herald-Traveler and
CHSNE collection.)

NUNS AND GIRLS IN PICNIC, 1950S. The
Maryknoll Sisters Center also organized
outdoor activities such as this picnic for
Chinese girls. The Catholic nuns are in
plainclothes with children playing in a camp.
(Courtesy of Lela Wong.)

CHINESE GIRL SCOUTS, C. 1960. The Maryknoll Sisters Center organized three Girl Scout troops—Troop 52 as a younger Brownie group, Troop 445 at the intermediate level, and Troop 551 (pictured here) as the most senior group. The Girl Scouts held regular meetings, elected officers, and earned merit badges for activities such as tree identification and cooking. They learned dances, went on camping trips, and learned how to build campfires for cooking. (Courtesy of Cynthia Yee.)

Five

WAR, NATIONALISM, AND CITIZENSHIP

VICTORY PARADE, 1945. Returning Chinese American soldiers were honored in the Double Ten Day (which celebrates the founding of the Republic of China on October 11, 1911) victory parade on October 10, 1945, after World War II. Members of both the Chinese Nationalist Party and the Chinese Merchants Association were out in full force to support Chinese American military personnel. (Courtesy of International Society.)

CHINESE SOLDIER IN WORLD WAR I, 1918. Do Gan Goon was born in 1893 in Toishan and came to the Boston area via Vancouver and Montreal in 1912. In 1918, he was drafted into the U.S. Army during World War I. Upon discharge in 1919, Do Gan Goon received his U.S. citizenship. Armed with his citizenship, he was able to return to China to marry Toy Len Goon. (Courtesy of Edward Guen and Maine Historical Society.)

CHINESE AMERICAN MILITARY FAMILY, 1940s. All three Yuu brothers served in the U.S. armed forces during World War II. The Yuu family is believed to be the only Chinese American family to have sent three sons to serve in World War II at the same time. Their father served under Gen. John J. Pershing in World War I. (Courtesy of Joseph Yuu and CHSNE collection.)

CHINESE IN 14TH AIR SERVICE GROUP, 1943. William Seam Wong was a member of the 14th Air Service Group, which provided logistical and maintenance support for combat units in south China during World War II. The photo album of the Flying Tigers unit documents his achievement. (Courtesy of William Seam Wong and CHSNE collection.)

CHINESE DEMONSTRATIONS AGAINST JAPAN, 1938. Chinese Americans demonstrated at the corner of Tyler and Beach Streets on July 7, 1938, in support of China against Japan's invasion. The Chinese banner carries the phrase "save the nation" with participants holding both American and Chinese flags. (Courtesy of CHSNE collection.)

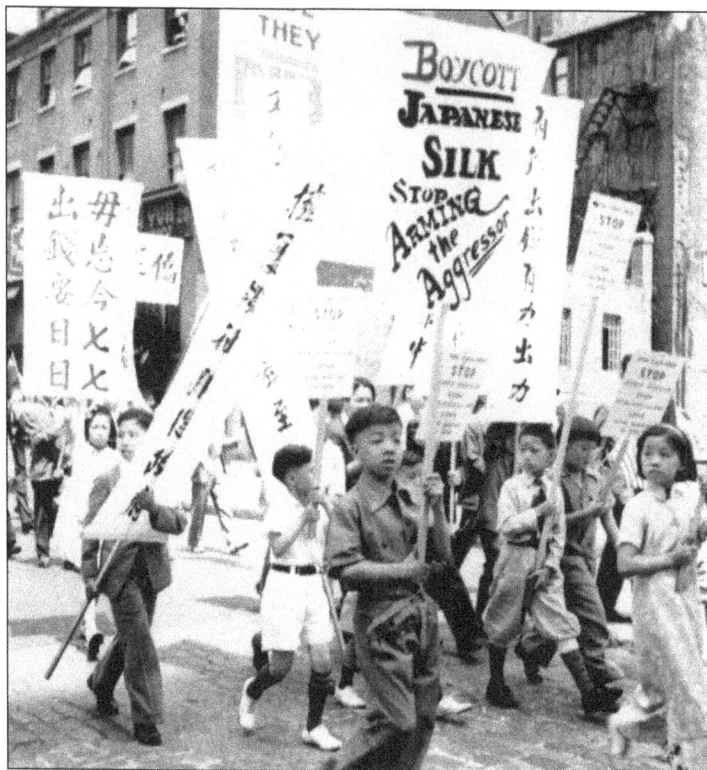

BOYCOTTING JAPANESE SILK, 1941. Chinese children participated in a demonstration urging the boycott of Japanese silk to protest Japan's invasion of China. The banners, in both English and Chinese, were carried by students of the Quong Kow Chinese School. (Courtesy of Tunney Lee.)

CRUSADE FOR CHILDREN, 1940s. Chinese store owners participated in appeals for donations in relief of war refugees during and after World War II. The donation drive pictured here occurred at the Chong Lung Kee grocery at 18 Hudson Street. (Courtesy of CHSNE collection.)

FUNDS FOR RELIEF FOR CHINESE REFUGEES, 1939. Raising large banners in both English and Chinese, Chinese residents in Boston organized a parade on Hudson Street advocating funds for relief for Chinese refugees. (Courtesy of Reggie Wong.)

SUPPORT OF AMERICAN TROOPS, 1941. Chinese demonstrators marched along Hudson Street in 1941, proudly displaying American flags in support of U.S. involvement in World War II. (Courtesy of Tunney Lee.)

Chinese Parade in Front of the Chinese Nationalist Party Office, 1940s. This parade was organized in front of the Chinese Nationalist Party headquarters on Hudson Street. One Chinese banner translates to "we will resist against Japan until the end." (Courtesy of CHSNE collection.)

Waiting for Madame Chiang, 1943. Families and children waited in the snow to greet Madame Chiang Kai-shek during her visit to Boston in March 1943. She came to the United States to appeal to Congress for extra funding in support of Chinese resistance against Japan. (Courtesy of International Society.)

WOMEN RAISE FUNDS FOR WAR EFFORT, 1940S. Ruby Foo's Den, Hudson Street, served as the backdrop for women raising money to support the Chinese war effort against Japan. The outstretched flag collected money tossed in by restaurant workers who responded to the appeal. (Courtesy of International Society.)

CHINESE MERCHANTS ASSOCIATION VICTORY BANQUET, 1945. After the atomic bombs were dropped and the Japanese were close to surrendering to the Allies, the Chinese Merchants Association hosted a victory banquet on August 14, 1945. (Courtesy of Catherine Mah.)

CHINESE AMERICAN VICTORY PARADE, 1945. The celebration of the victory of China and the Allied Powers in the Pacific War reached its climax on the national day of the Republic of China, October 10, 1945. Chinatown held a spectacular victory parade. Spectators and parade floats overflowed the streets as part of celebrations that lasted for months. (Courtesy of International Society.)

CHINESE CONSOLIDATED BENEVOLENT ASSOCIATION VICTORY BANQUET, 1945. A grand victory banquet was held by the Chinese Consolidated Benevolent Association of New England on October 10, 1945, on the national day of the Republic of China. The event filled the famous Bradford Hotel with hundreds of participants from various family associations. (Courtesy of Lela Wong.)

BOSTON CHINATOWN AMERICAN LEGION BANQUET, 1945. The Boston Chinatown American Legion Post No. 328 held its own banquet and dance to mark its first installation, at Hotel Bradford on December 21, 1945. (Courtesy of Catherine Mah.)

CHILDREN HEAR ABOUT NEWS OF JAPAN DEFEAT, 1945. Chinatown children hold up newspapers on the eve of the Japanese surrender and the Allied victory in the Pacific War on August 14, 1945. The racial epithets against Japan in the newspapers reflected the intense animosities towards the enemy. (Courtesy of Bill Chin.)

PURCHASE OF U.S. SAVINGS BONDS, 1945. Chinese children participated in a Chinatown rally encouraging the purchase of U.S. savings bonds during World War II. Children are dressed in traditional clothing and pose in front of an American flag. (Courtesy of International Society.)

QUINCY SCHOOL CIVICS LESSONS, 1946. Chinese children at the Quincy School learned about China and world geography in a class on February 8, 1946. Posters and flyers displayed information about Chinese leaders as well as scenes relating to China. (Courtesy of International Society.)

PLEDGE OF ALLEGIANCE BY CHINESE STUDENTS, 1946. Chinese American students pledged allegiance at the Quincy School in Chinatown in 1946. The number of Chinese students increased considerably after World War II, a part of the overall American baby boom. (Courtesy of International Society.)

Six

URBAN RENEWAL AND ACCULTURATION

CHINESE MERCHANTS ASSOCIATION BUILDING, 1963. Construction of the Central Artery and the Massachusetts Turnpike Extension resulted in the Chinese Merchants Association building being reduced in size by one-third, only a few years after the building was newly constructed. (Courtesy of CHSNE collection; photograph by Joseph Dennehy.)

NEW CHINESE MERCHANTS ASSOCIATION, 1951. The Chinese Merchants Association building at 20 Hudson Street was a new landmark for Boston Chinatown during its completion and dedication in 1951. With its traditional roof pagoda, impressive facade of balconies, and side lanterns, the building represented a visible entrance to Chinatown. (Courtesy of CHSNE collection.)

OPENING CEREMONY OF CHINESE MERCHANTS ASSOCIATION, 1951. The dedication of the building on October 2, 1951, drew numerous spectators and visitors to Chinatown. The festive atmosphere was indicative of the growth of the Chinese community during the postwar years. (Courtesy of Reggie Wong.)

PROTEST AGAINST CENTRAL ARTERY PROJECT, 1954. With the construction of the Southeast Expressway in 1954, the city attempted to remove the entire Chinese Merchants Association building that had been completed just three years earlier. Wong Jayne, a Chinatown leader, is seen here affixing his signature to a petition being signed by thousands of residents asking Gov. Christian Herter to change the projected Central Artery's route. As planned, the route would have eliminated a huge swath of Chinatown and the existing garment district. (Courtesy of Boston Traveler/International Society.)

NEW LOOK OF THE MERCHANTS ASSOCIATION, 1956. Since the highway project required partial demolition of the Albany Street side of the Chinese Merchants Association building, the association lost over a third of its floor space. The balconies facing Hudson Street were enclosed with glass and a metal grid in an attempt to regain some of the lost space. (Courtesy of CHSNE collection.)

HUDSON STREET BEFORE URBAN RENEWAL, 1953. This photograph was taken prior to the demolition of Hudson Street homes and businesses. Three- and four-story brick tenement houses lined both sides of the street. Because of community concerns, instead of taking all of Hudson Street, the eastern side from Kneeland Street to Broadway was torn down to construct an entrance ramp for the Massachusetts Turnpike. Those residents who were forced to relocate received very limited compensation. The bitterness left by the state's actions still lingers today. (Courtesy of International Society.)

CHILDREN IN THE HUDSON STREET NEIGHBORHOOD, LATE 1940s. Reggie and Caroline Wong, brother and sister, play and pose in front of the tenements of Hudson Street. It was a close-knit neighborhood where every school child knew each other by name or nickname. (Courtesy of Reggie Wong.)

HUDSON STREET BUILDING DEMOLITION, 1963. All of Albany Street and one side of Hudson Street, south of Kneeland Street, were demolished after 1963 to make room for the Massachusetts Turnpike Extension. The demolition on Hudson Street added fuel to a growing antihighway movement as the public began to question the price exacted on the neighborhoods and inhabitants. (Courtesy of CHSNE collection.)

WESTERN WEDDING, 1940. Tony and Amy Wing held a lavish wedding at the First Baptist Church on Commonwealth Avenue in Boston in February 1940. The bridal party includes the budding architect I. M. Pei. (Courtesy of Amy Wing.)

WEDDING PHOTOGRAPH IN BELFAST, MAINE, 1940. The father of the bride, Hing Wong, lived in Maine for many years but then moved to Boston during World War II, as did the bride's brother, John Wong. Despite the distance, many Chinese settlers in Maine and New Hampshire perceived Boston Chinatown as a social and cultural center of New England. (Courtesy of Gary Libby.)

FAMILY OF DO GAN AND TOY LEN GOON, 1941. The Goon couple, described earlier as the World War I veteran and the Mother of the Year, is photographed here in Maine with their eight children. After Do Gan's death, Toy Len Goon raised her children as a single parent and eventually moved to Boston with her eight children in 1952. (Courtesy of Edward and Amy Guen.)

GUNG HO CLUB LION DANCE, 1950S. The Gung Ho Club was founded in 1948 by a group of eight Chinese teenagers seeking an alternative to the Chinatown YMCA, which at the time was the only social and athletic facility in the Chinese community. Translated from Chinese, *gung ho* means "working together." (Courtesy of Reggie Wong.)

113

CHINESE PARADE ON HUDSON STREET, 1954. Chinese organizations appeared in full force for the community's Double Ten Celebration in 1954, including the Gung Ho Athletic Club (front) and the Quong Kow junior high school band (back). To the left is the headquarters of the Chinese Nationalist Party; to the right is the House of Wong restaurant. (Courtesy of Helen Chin Schlichte.)

YMCA Building, 1960s. The Chinatown YMCA, founded by missionary efforts in the late 19th century, occupied this small building for over 30 years. Its second floor boarding rooms accommodated single male workers in the laundry and restaurant trade who had left their families behind in China. The Wang YMCA, as it is now known, provided sports activities and leisure programs for adults as well as youth in its limited spaces. Before relocating to a newer facility on Washington Street in the 1990s, the Y was housed in a temporary inflated structure, known as the "Bubble," for 30 years. (Courtesy of International Society.)

MARYKNOLL LIONS BASKETBALL TEAM, 1946–1947. Two Catholic priests affiliated with the Maryknoll Sisters Center helped organize a basketball team, the Maryknoll Lions, immediately after the center opened in 1946. This is the first team photograph, taken at the Maryknoll Sisters Center. (Courtesy of Lela Wong.)

CHINESE BASEBALL GAME ON THE PARKING LOT, 1948. The parking lot at the corner of Beach and Kingston Streets, now the site of the Chinatown Park of the Rose Kennedy Greenway, served as a baseball field on Sundays prior to the construction of the Central Artery. (Courtesy of International Society.)

SPECTATORS OF STREET SOFTBALL, 1948. Spectators often watched baseball games in parking lots in the late 1940s, as recreational open space within Chinatown was nonexistent. The spectators included Chinese and non-Chinese alike. (Courtesy of International Society.)

CHINESE YOUTH VOLLEYBALL, 1970. Volleyball was and continues to be a major sport among Chinese youth. Every Labor Day weekend, Boston joins other North American Chinatown communities in a highly competitive tournament. In this 1970 photograph, Boston hosted the North American Invitational Volleyball Tournament on the Tyler Street parking lot. (Courtesy of CHSNE collection.)

CHINESE CHRISTIAN CHURCH OF NEW ENGLAND, 1970s. The Chinese Christian Church was the first active postwar Protestant church to offer services in the community. It was located on Harvard Street from the 1950s to the 1970s when this mural on its facade calling for "love" was created. The church later moved to a suburban location. Some of its church leaders formed the Boston Chinese Evangelical Church to maintain a presence in Boston Chinatown. (Courtesy of International Society.)

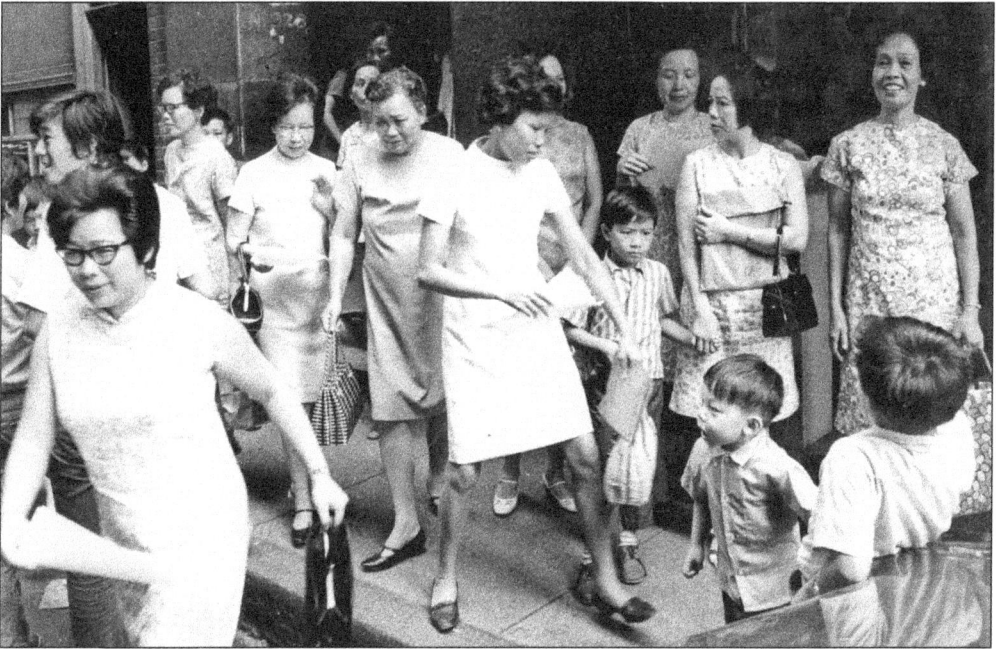

NEW IMMIGRANTS FROM HONG KONG, 1970. Mothers rush to pick up their children finishing their early evening classes at the Kwong Kow Chinese School. As more families immigrated to Boston from Hong Kong, they brought with them their Hong Kong sense of style and fashion. (Courtesy of CHSNE collection.)

CHINESE FEMALE GARMENT WORKER, 1972. The Chinese community shared its neighborhood with the garment industry. Consequently, many women found jobs in the garment factories following World War II up to the late 1970s, when the garment industry in Boston declined. (Courtesy of Boston Globe; photograph by Charles Nixon.)

NEW HOUSING FOR CHINATOWN, 1970s. After 1965, when the immigration laws were changed to allow for family reunification, there was a surge of new Chinese immigrants to the community. City planners worked with the community and other government agencies to create much-needed housing, including projects such as the Tai Tung Village, shown here, and the Mass Pike Towers. (Courtesy of International Society.)

CHINATOWN PUBLIC HEARING, 1969. Representatives from the City of Boston listen to citizens describing community concerns. The grievance hearing eventually led to the addition of a city office known as the Chinatown Little City Hall by the mayor of Boston to coordinate city services with the neighborhood. (Courtesy of International Society; photograph by Tom Croke.)

Seven

REMEMBERING THE PAST

CHINATOWN GATE, 1982. The idea of a Chinatown gate in Boston was conceived in the 1970s to create an official symbol of Chinatown. Boston joined San Francisco, Chicago, Philadelphia, and Washington, D.C., as one of the few American cities that has erected an official gate for its Chinatown. The gate, which took a decade to complete due to limited funding and technical difficulties before its dedication in 1982, stands at the intersection of Beach Street and Surface Road. One side of the gate is engraved with a phrase by Dr. Sun Yat-sen that reads "All under Heaven is for the good of the people." The other side is engraved with the Confucian virtues of "propriety, righteousness, honesty, and integrity." (Courtesy of CHSNE collection.)

MOUNT HOPE CEMETERY, 1990S. Many Chinese "bachelors" in Boston who died from the 1920s to 1960s are buried in all-Chinese sections of Mount Hope Cemetery in the Mattapan section of Boston. In the 1980s, two Chinese community leaders, Davis Woo and David S. Y. Wong, were concerned about the upkeep of these Chinese burial grounds and wanted to find a way to remember their ancestors in a proper way. They helped lead efforts to found the Chinese Historical Society of New England in order to restore the burial ground and build a new altar. Pictured is the old altar at the cemetery. (Courtesy of Peter Kiang.)

CHINESE IMMIGRANT MEMORIAL, 2007. With the dedication of volunteers from the Chinese Historical Society of New England, support and grants from the Boston Parks and Recreation Department and Browne Fund, as well as funding from Chinatown organizations and community donations, the work begun 18 years earlier by Messrs Woo and Wong, and continued by Bik-Fung Ng and Deborah Dong, came to fruition when the new Boston Chinese Immigrant Memorial was completed in 2007. Sitting on the site of the old crumbling altar, the new memorial is engraved with three Chinese phrases: "Remembering those who came before you," "Long rivers flow from distant origins" (signifying the long journey of the immigrants from China to Boston), and "Deep roots nourish abundant leaves" (signifying that the Chinese have settled here and future generations have the opportunity to flourish here, thanks to the legacy of those buried at Mount Hope Cemetery). (Courtesy of Deborah Dong.)

MOUNT HOPE IMMIGRANT MEMORIAL OPENING CEREMONY, 2007. On a sunny day in March 2007, community members and City of Boston officials gathered at Mount Hope Cemetery to unveil the new Boston Chinese Immigrant Memorial designed by architect Jookun Lim. Here, members of the Gee How Oak Tin Association pose with Davis Woo (first row, ninth from left) in front of the new community altar at the memorial. (Author's collection.)

CHINATOWN MURAL, 1986. The Chinatown community mural, originally located at 36 Oak Street in Boston Chinatown, was a project initiated by the Quincy School Community Council (now known as BCNC). The mural depicts the history and perseverance of the Chinese settlement in Boston from its origins in the 19th century to the present. The images of the mural include workers in laundries, restaurants, garment factories; growth of families and communities; and civil rights struggles among Chinese Americans in recent decades. Hundreds of people helped design and paint the mural. The mural was on the wall of the Boston Chinatown Neighborhood Center (BCNC) for 16 years until it was torn down in 2002. To pay tribute to the history of the community BCNC created a replica of the mural in the lobby of its new home at 38 Ash Street in 2005. (Courtesy of Carmen Chan and CHSNE collection.)

OXFORD PLACE, 2006. Oxford Place today is a reminder of the historical past of the original Chinese settlement in Boston, both in terms of the preservation of its original streetscape and the less-than-ideal living conditions in a sunless narrow alley. (Courtesy of Deborah Dong.)

HARRISON AVENUE, 2006. The balcony above the Eldo bakery on Harrison Avenue and the tile mosaic in front of the entrance of the building are remarkable for their historical significance. They are located at the earliest commercial block of 19th-century Chinatown. While the middle of the block from 34 to 38 Harrison Avenue has preserved its historic character, the building at the corner of Beach Street is now being converted into a new condominium. The challenges of historical preservation lie ahead. (Courtesy of Deborah Dong.)

EAST MEETS WEST, 2006. The traditional streetscape and facade of the Lee Family Association on 10 Tyler Street stand in front of high-rise apartments and office buildings. The office tower in the background is One Lincoln Center, built in 2002. Its investors included a group of Chinese businesspeople who donated some of their proceeds to community organizations in Chinatown. Perhaps the future of Boston Chinatown will be a mixture of modern development and ongoing preservation of traditional streetscapes. (Courtesy of Deborah Dong.)

BIBLIOGRAPHY

Asian Community Development Corporation. *A Chinatown Banquet: Exploring Boston Chinatown*. Boston: Mike Blockstein and the Asian Community Development Corporation, 2006.

Boston 200 Corporation. *Chinatown*. The Boston Neighborhood History Series 4. Boston: Self published, 1976.

Chan, Shehong. "Reconstructing the Chinese American Experience in Lowell, Massachusetts, 1870s–1970s." Institute for Asian American Studies, University of Massachusetts Boston, 2003.

Chapman, Mary. "Notes on the Chinese in Boston." *Journal of American Folklore* V. no. 19, (1892): 321–324.

Chu, Doris C. J. *Chinese in Massachusetts: Their Experiences and Contributions*. Boston: Chinese Culture Institute, 1987.

Fan, Stephanie. "Boston Chinatown since 1872: Growth and Changes." *Chinese Historical Society of New England Newsletter*. Vol. 8, no. 1, Fall 2002.

Heywood, Herbert. "Chinese in New England." *New England Magazine* XXVII, (June 1905): 473–483.

Krim, Arthur. *Chinatown-South Cove: Final Survey Report*. Boston: Boston Landmarks Commission, 1997.

Li, Giles and Peter Kiang. "The 1903 Immigration Raid in Boston Chinatown." *Chinese Historical Society of New England Newsletter*. Vol. 10, no. 1, Fall 2004.

Libby, Gary. "Chinese in Maine." *Chinese Historical Society of New England Newsletter*. Vol. 9. no. 1, Fall 2003.

Lo, Shauna. "Challenging Exclusion: Chinese Entering the Northeast." Chinese Historical Society of New England Newsletter, Vol. 9, no. 1, Fall 2003.

Murphey, Rhoads. "Boston's Chinatown," in *Economic Geography*. Vol. 28, no. 3, (1952): 244–255.

Sullivan, Charles. *The Chinese in Boston, 1970*. Boston: Action for Boston Community Development, 1970.

To, Wing-kai. "Two Accounts of Early Boston Chinatown in 1892 and 1905." *Chinese Historical Society of New England Newsletter*. Vol. 11, no. 1, Fall 2005.

———. "Ninety Years of Chinese Language and Heritage Education in the Kwong Kow School." *Chinese Historical Society of New England Newsletter*. Vol. 12, no. 1, Fall 2006.

Tom, May Lee. "Remembering Hudson Street." *Chinese Historical Society of New England Newsletter*. Vol. 2, no. 1, Spring 1996.

Wong, K. Scott. "The Eagle Seeks a Helpless Quarry: The 1903 Boston Chinatown Raid Revisited" *Amerasia Journal*. Vol. 22, no. 3, (1996): 81–103.

Visit us at
arcadiapublishing.com

www.ingramcontent.com/pod-product-compliance
Lightning Source LLC
Chambersburg PA
CBHW080611110426
42813CB00006B/1473